Successfully Defeat Pain & Grief

One Man's Journey Through Significant Loss

JAMES MENTZER

Copyright © 2022 by James Mentzer

All rights reserved. No part of this book may be used or reproduced by any means, graphic, electronic or mechanical, including photocopying, recording, taping or by any information storage retrieval system, without the written permission of the author, except in the case of brief quotations embodied in reviews.

Paperback ISBN 978-1-945169-76-2
eBook ISBN 978-1-945169-77-9

Published by
Orison Publishers, Inc.
PO Box 188, Grantham, PA 17027
www.OrisonPublishers.com

Acknowledgments

In loving memory of my wife, Debbie Mentzer, and my mother and father, Doris and James Mentzer, for without their love and support I wouldn't be the person I am today. I thank my brother and his wife, Tim and Connie Mentzer; my brothers-in-law and their wives, Don and Linda Rutz and Barry and Bonnie Rutz; my uncles and aunts, John and Janet Mentzer and Bob and Helen Fisher; and my cousins and nephews for their love and support. Also, thanks to my church family and friends, and Pastors Chris and Rachel Swab, for their support and care.

A special thank you goes to Ron James and Marsan James Grasty for showing me that life was worth living and that I had a story to share.

Thanks also go to Lamar Kukuk and Krina Agnew for their work and time to make sure this book became a beautiful story about my life and the three people whom I loved very much, as it will keep their memory alive for a long time.

Contents

Prologue vii
Chapter One Childhood, Christmas and the Campground 1
Chapter Two Something Missing, Something Found 23
Chapter Three A Turn for the Worse 47
Chapter Four Then, the Rains Came 67
Chapter Five You Are Not Alone 85

PROLOGUE
I Remember

Her name was Debbie.

She was my wife. We were married for twenty-four years. A nurse's aide, she worked at Carlisle Hospital for more than thirty years. We'd see the patients out in public. They'd remember her after their surgeries and thank her for the care she gave them. Debbie liked to go to the movies and watch Westerns on TV. She loved *Walker, Texas Ranger* and had all the episodes on DVD. She was a big Pittsburgh Steelers fan and taught me a lot about the game. She liked to bake; she made great angel food cake and cookies at Christmastime. Debbie was an outgoing, positive person who always found the brighter side. She brought me around to the positive in life.

It was November 17, 2020, around one o'clock in the morning, when I got the call. She had COVID and had fought so hard for a week, but now they were going to put her on the ventilator. They said that it wouldn't be long now, that I should stay close to the phone. I got another call later that night. She was dying. I think I just kept repeating "no ... no ... no" the whole time. Yelling. Crying out.

I thought my life was over.

* * *

Her name was Doris.

She was my mother. Mom was a music teacher until I and my brother were born, and then when we graduated, she substituted and taught music again. She played the piano for the church and liked classical music. Mother made the most wonderful Christmas dinners and invited the whole family over. She beat cancer twice. I saw how she fought and kept coming back, and she gave me that fight. Mom was great at giving hugs.

It was November 18, 2020, when my brother Tim called and told me that our mother had died. She was in a nursing home in Lancaster, Pennsylvania, across from where he lived. My father lived with her in the same assisted living apartment. Tim actually knew that Mom was dying the day before, the day my wife died, but he didn't tell me. He didn't want to put that burden on me.

It would have been too hard.

* * *

His name was James.

He was my father. He was James Mentzer, Sr. He and my mother ran the Dogwood Acres Campground for thirty years. We'd ride around together and fix things. He taught me a lot about maintenance, and we'd go on equipment runs together. My father used to like to have a cookout on Father's Day, to have the whole family together. He was a teacher, too, of social studies. When he was younger, we had a farm with cows and pigs, and I wanted to be a farmer when I grew up. He went through cancer as well.

It was February 6, 2021, when the hospital called me. They couldn't find Tim. Dad had trouble breathing and couldn't catch his breath after dialysis. They did the tests and found out that he had COVID, too. He died that day, and I had to tell Tim.

I had to be the strong one that day.

* * *

My wife, my mother and my father all died within ninety days. I reached out for help when the situation grew beyond me. God helped me to find the right people to help me. I fought to go on after they died because I knew that's what they'd want, for me to enjoy my life again. I know they're cheering me on, every step of the way.

Now, more than anything, I want people to know who they were and how I was able to go through the pain and grief. Things happen, but you can still come around and choose life and start looking ahead. It's not an easy road. You have to fight. But it's worth it. It's worth it now.

I've started to remember the happy moments now. And I want to share them with you.

CHAPTER ONE
Childhood, Christmas and the Campground

Country Life
I've lived in Newville, Pennsylvania, for fifty-five years, all my life. It's a borough of about thirteen hundred people near Carlisle. And if you don't know where Carlisle is, that's near Harrisburg.

Newville only has one red light, so it's a real quiet town. Actually, we didn't live "in" town, but more out in the country. I grew up in a beautiful, quiet setting, a really rural area. The houses nearby didn't have their own post office, so you thought of the whole area as Newville. It was a farming community, the kind where if you need any help, your neighbors come and help you.

It's still that way today. My neighbors come and plow the snow for me in the winter and don't ask anything for it. You can offer, but they say they don't want anything. That's just what a neighbor does.

Growing up, it was me, my parents, and my younger brother Tim. Tim and I had a really good childhood together and did a lot of things I enjoyed. We were always close. A lot of kids at school thought we were twins because we looked a lot alike. We were a year apart in school at first, but later I ended up staying back a year and then we were in the same grade. You could say that was so we'd be closer together. Mom kidded me about that. I always knew he had my back. Me and Tim always liked to joke around together. He was the one who could always make everybody laugh.

When my parents first moved onto the farm property, there was an old farmhouse there, but they wanted to build something bigger so they could start a family. That farmhouse still exists today. They sold it to someone else, and those owners fixed it all up.

My parents introduced me to Christ through church, making sure Tim and I got to St. Peter's Lutheran Church in Newville every Sunday and sending us to Sunday school. On Sunday morning we'd get up, have eggs and bacon or something like that for breakfast, and then get dressed up for church, putting on our Sunday best. We had our shoes shined.

Sunday school was usually first. When we were younger, my mother played the piano for the kids downstairs before Sunday school, and we'd sing all those great songs like "Jesus Loves Me."

> *Jesus loves me! This I know,*
> *For the Bible tells me so;*
> *Little ones to Him belong;*
> *They are weak, but He is strong.*[1]

What really helped is when we got to catechism class and understood what the whole meaning of church was. I really wanted to go to church then because I knew what it was all about. I remember the pastor talking to my parents afterwards, and he told them that I really seemed to understand what it was all about. That made them very proud.

I wanted to be a farmer when I grew up; that was my first dream. My father had cows and pigs when I was young, and I loved the outdoors. I'd help my dad out on the farm; I couldn't wait to do that kind of work with him. I learned to drive the tractors and other vehicles, and if he was going to go somewhere for other equipment, he'd take me with him, so we'd spend that time together.

I remember driving to Carlisle with him. We'd pass all these empty fields with no houses. He'd say, "They're going to build all this up

---

1 Anna Bartlett Warner, "Jesus Loves Me," 1859, public domain.

someday," and that's exactly what happened. Today all that farmland are businesses. The change took away a lot of the countryside I remember, but luckily there is still a lot of farmland around Newville.

One year, my parents took on the cows of our neighbors, who went to work in Alaska for a while. My favorite part was that I got to see calves born. That was a beautiful experience. It was wonderful to watch the calves grow into cows.

We had two dogs, Blackie and Brownie. Tim and I were responsible for feeding and taking care of them. They were outside dogs, so you'd take the food and water to them. Out in the country, though, you could let them take a run and they would always come back home. One of them had puppies, and my mother had a great picture of her sitting in a Radio Flyer wagon holding the whole litter.

We had horses for a year or so around when I was five. I remember my cousin came up to visit and rode a horse like you're supposed to. It looked pretty easy. Then I tried, and a snake came up. The horse threw me off.

My parents gave me an appreciation of nature that I still have to this day. However, it was my Aunt Helen who picked me up when the horse threw me and made sure I was okay.

Aunt Helen was my mother's older sister. Mom used to tell the story of how the two of them would fight as kids over who would wash the dishes. My grandmother would walk up to them and, whichever one was talking, stick the dishcloth in her mouth. My mother always insisted that it was Aunt Helen who got the dishcloth the most.

I don't know if I believe that or not.

I remember how Mom got sick of us brothers arguing over who was going to wash the dishes. One day my parents said, "Guess what we bought today?" Tim and I both said, "A dishwasher?" But it was just a Chevy Impala, one of those big ones from back in the day. We didn't want the car; we wanted the dishwasher! Eventually Mom did get one of those, too.

We grew up on organic food long before organic was a thing. My mother had a backyard garden and grew blueberries, tomatoes, potatoes—mostly everything.

I remember one day, when she was out working in the garden, Tim and I were fighting over a bottle of soda we were supposed to be sharing. We each wanted more than the other and ended up throwing it at each other, getting soda all over the kitchen. We didn't notice she was outside until she came in the door. We knew we were in trouble. We both looked at the other like "It wasn't me!" Mom gave us "That Look" and let us hear about it, too!

Our family went to Florida one year when we were kids. Our parents took us to Disney World. Because we were so young, I only remember bits and pieces of being there. The one thing I'll always remember about that trip is our parents told us Florida was warm, so we didn't take any coats or anything. And when we got there, it was freezing cold!

Our town, Newville, has the Cumberland Drive-In movie theater, which opened in 1952. My parents used to take us there when we were younger. The first movie I remember seeing there was *Bambi*. It was a big deal!

Living in the country, we had a fishing pond. My brother and I were best friends and would go fishing together in the summer. My paternal grandparents Dorothy and Sheldon Mentzer would come by, and our grandmother would be there with us a lot when we fished. Tim and I didn't like putting the worms on the hooks, so she helped us with that. It seemed kind of cruel, but they were slimy and slithering around, and I didn't like it! It was a small pond, about four feet deep, but we could catch lots of sunfish. One time my grandmother talked my parents into cooking up those fish, but they were all bones because they were so small. That was the last time we did that!

Sometimes there'd be ducks on the pond—snapping turtles, too. One year there was a turtle that got really aggressive and came up on the porch of my parents' house! We'd see raccoons around as well.

We had tons of fun when our cousins Bill and Robin would come stay with our grandparents. Bill was a couple of years older than us, and Robin was a couple of years younger. It all worked out, and we usually had a good time. However, we were closer to Robin since, as Bill got older, he didn't want to play as much as she did. We were typical country kids, making mud pies, digging in the dirt and searching for whatever we could find. Tim and I would put a sandbox in the mud sometimes and pretend it was a boat.

Robin would ask my mom if she could go swimming in the pond and Mom would say "no," but then we just went someplace where Mom couldn't hear and swam anyway. Actually, we kind of walked into the pond. It wasn't very deep. But it was nice and cool in the summer.

Grandfather Sheldon and I were best friends. Most people called him Buck because of all the deer hunting he did. We'd sit on the porch at night and talk. He was a good listener, and I was happy to have someone to share things with. He always seemed relaxed when I was around him. We'd sit on the porch in the summertime, watch the scenery and just talk. You could see the pond from there.

He always made time for me, and that time was very special.

Sometimes we'd stay with my grandparents when my parents went into town and ran errands. My grandmother would make us a kid's meal like hot dogs and French fries. Sometimes she'd go shopping with Mother, giving her a chance to get out of the house. She also taught Bible school, and I'd go along with her to that.

My other grandfather on my mom's side, Harvey Hein, always took us for haircuts. The exciting thing about those trips was that the barber had the old-time soda machine with the bottles and the bottle opener on the side. That type of machine was going out of style at the time, but those glass bottles really kept the soda cold!

The convenience store was about a ten-minute drive from our home because we were out in the country. When we were out and about in public, Mother always made sure that we held the doors for people. And if somebody did something special for us, she made sure that we thanked that person. To this day, I'm always proud when someone calls me a gentleman.

Our parents gave us an allowance, which we earned by doing chores like feeding the dogs and cleaning our rooms, so that we could pick out things we wanted when we went to the store. We collected Matchbox cars and were both allowed to pick out one every time we were there. The metal Matchbox cars with doors that could open were the best.

We only had three TV channels, and since our parents limited our time with TV, we had to find other things to do. Tim and I were more outside kids, not having the TV on all the time. I'm kind of still like that today.

Twister was a game we always liked to play. You could do that with the whole family. We'd play Monopoly; that game took forever. Then there was Headache, where you'd push the plastic popper to roll the dice and then move your little cones around the board. When we got older, Tim and I had a three-wheeler, and we'd ride around together.

There was always something to do. We were never bored.

My dad instilled responsibility in me through work and my mother with support. Her being strong like that made me strong like I am now. When I started looking for a wife, I was looking for someone to have a partnership with like my parents had in their marriage. They were always there for each other, and they always liked to do things together. My dad had more of a sense of humor, although my mom had a pretty good one, too. In our house, we had to say our prayers before we went to bed and before each meal, and I still do so today.

Dad could be firm; when he gave you "That Look," you knew you were in trouble. I could push the boundaries, wanting my freedom to do things I wasn't quite ready for yet. But Mom was good at jumping in and smoothing things over when it got serious.

As a music teacher, Mom loved classical music; it was always the classics for her. She played piano, and she played for the church. Dad wasn't really a music person. One thing I'd learn along the way, there's a lot of give and take in a marriage.

Holidays and Snow Days

We had a Halloween parade in town every year, and Tim and I went trick or treating. Because we lived in the country, it was mostly to our church group that we'd go looking for candy. My parents would drive us so we could knock on the doors. Mom made our costumes. She'd go into a bag of old material she kept and would always find something that worked. One year I remember dressing as a pirate. I think that was my favorite costume.

For our birthdays, she'd make the special meal we liked. For me, the special meal was this corned beef loaf that had potatoes and other items in it along with a crust that was really good. There'd be a vegetable, too, but I wasn't a big vegetable eater.

Then there was the birthday cake. Angel food with pudding in it was her specialty. That recipe was passed down to her from my great aunt. My grandmother was a little jealous that her sister chose to share that recipe with my mom, I think. Not only was the cake delicious, but Mom also would make them in special shapes for our birthdays. She did a lot of special things like that for us, always with extra love and care.

For Easter, my parents would hide the baskets from us; we'd have to look for them in the morning when we got up. Well, actually it was when *they* got up, since we were only allowed to start looking for the baskets once they were awake. We'd have breakfast afterwards—hot cross buns that my mother made—so we'd have to wait to eat the candy. It could be torture to wait with that candy right there in front of us!

Then we got ready for church with the new outfits we received for Easter. We went along to the store, but Mom would pick the suits out and then we'd get fitted. At the church, the kids would have an Easter procession where we put flowers on the cross. I wasn't too nervous because my mind was still on the Easter basket! Mom would help to play for the procession, with her on the piano and another person playing on the organ.

After church we had Easter dinner with my grandparents. My parents had a dining room for when guests came. They pulled out all the good china for that day. We had ham and mashed potatoes for dinner. Mom would have a gelatin salad, too.

Then we'd finally get to the basket. I went for the peanut butter eggs first. We had the chocolate rabbit and the marshmallow Peeps. Back then, there was only one color—yellow. The candy all looked so nice sitting in the artificial grass of the basket.

Christmas was my favorite holiday as a child. My mother loved decorating the Christmas tree, and we helped her. We always put on the tinsel and then a star on top of the tree. When we were younger, we had a little tree for us to decorate, too. My parents had a dining room and the regular living room. They put our little tree in the living room and the "good tree" in the dining room because there's where all the guests would come in.

The church service I always looked forward to was the Christmas Eve service, which was an indoor candlelight service. The neat thing was, since our church was a small church, everyone was involved in decorating the church for Christmas. The kids would get to stage the Nativity scene.

On Christmas morning, Tim and I would wake up early and wait for my parents to get up. Of course, they made us wait; we couldn't open anything until they got up and came downstairs. They'd make homemade cinnamon rolls for breakfast, and then it was time to start opening gifts!

As a kid, it was always fun to look through the Sears and Roebuck catalog around Christmastime and dream. I remember one year I really wanted this Tonka truck with a fifth wheel that went behind it, and my parents got it for me. Tim and I gave them a homemade card. Mom loved those cards because they came from the heart.

Mother made the most wonderful Christmas dinners and invited the whole family over. We had ham for Christmas; she'd do the whole spread, with all the trimmings. I remember especially the pecan pie she'd make. For Dad's birthday, she would make his favorite pumpkin pie.

My mother also baked a bunch of cookies. There was one kind she made with marshmallow, chocolate and peanut butter that was really good. We also made sugar cookies and decorated them with the different colors for Christmas. She let us help with making them, too. We used the cookie cutters and added sprinkles. Back in the 1970s, we'd have these big snowstorms that would close the roads for weeks. I remember going down to watch the snowplow, and the snow was higher than the plow itself. The road crew didn't have heavy equipment to move the snow then, just the plow, so you could get snowed in for weeks on end. When we had a snow day from school, my parents would take us out riding snowmobiles down the closed roads.

My parents got their snowmobiles in the summer, so they first tried them out in the yard without any snow. My aunt and uncle came up to check out the snowmobiles. My aunt got on the back and didn't say much. But we could tell she was scared when it took off really fast! Our neighbors had snowmobiles, too, and my parents would go out riding with them.

When we were younger, my father would pull my brother and I on a sled behind the three-wheeler over the ice. You could just go flying across that frozen pond on a sled. Dad could be a real kid at heart with us when it came to playing outside like that. When we got a little older, we'd ride that three-wheeler on the ice and go around in circles.

My parents would ride the snowmobiles alongside us, but one time my mother was too worried watching us to make sure we didn't get hurt and ended up flipping her snowmobile and hurting her shoulder. My parents had been doing those circles, too, before she realized there might be some danger to that. None of us were thinking about safety at first! I remember the doctor saying to her, "What are you doing, driving a snowmobile at that age!"

I was about twelve.

My father used to tell the story of a time when he took a bulldozer out on a frozen lake to clear off the snow for a youth group activity. The bulldozer went right through the ice and down into the water. That story became a joke after a while, but I bet it wasn't funny that day!

My parents had a big woodstove in the basement—that's where you'd come in to warm up. We'd take all the wet winter clothes and hang them up down there. Mom would make hot chocolate with marshmallows, and sometimes she offered cookies, too, depending on what time of year it was.

What wonderful memories.

Summertime at the Campground

In the summertime, my parents ran the Dogwood Acres campground in Newville which they built on the farm. They started the campground so there would be income after my mother gave up being a music teacher to stay home and take care of us. Mom had a full-time job taking care of the family and all the finances; she was like our accountant.

The camp was open on weekends for overnight campers during the summer. On holidays, the campers got three days. There was a big wooden sign my mother carved that greeted the campers. We had to paint it every year.

Mother loved dogwood trees, and she loved this poem about them:

When Christ was on earth, the dogwood grew
To a towering size with a lovely hue.
Its branches were strong and interwoven
And for Christ's cross its timbers were chosen.

Being distressed at the use of the wood
Christ made a promise which still holds good:

"Not ever again shall the dogwood grow
To be large enough for such a tree, and so
Slender and twisted it shall always be
With cross-shaped blossoms for all to see.

"The petals shall have bloodstains marked brown
And in the blossom's center a thorny crown.
All who see it will think of me,
Nailed to a cross from a dogwood tree.
Protected and cherished this tree shall be
A reflection to all of my agony."[2]

In the end, my parents ran the campground for thirty years before selling it. As of this writing, the new owners are coming up on twenty years of running it.

A mixture of people would come to the campground. In the summer, a lot of people who were traveling would show up for a weekend, pulling their campers. Then we had seasonals, people who came every year. They'd pay for the site for the whole year, leave their camper there, and then just come in the summer. Business was better some years than others. Sometimes we had great weather and a lot of campers; other years we might have rain and lose a lot of those weekends.

---

2 Author Unknown, "The Dogwood Tree," accessed November 15, 2021, http://mrmom.amaonline.com/Special/dogwoodtree.htm.

Back then, the campers didn't have all of the extras in them that they have now. A camper had a table, chairs and a bed to sleep in. You were lucky if you had air conditioning. It was an adventure!

We didn't have any seasonal employees. My parents did all of the work on their own. That's probably why they were so worn out when they got older. But they were very supportive of each other and worked well together, each doing what he and she was good at. They got us to help out, too. Sometimes as kids you didn't want that hard work, but that's normal. We were expected to work, so there wasn't a "no" option.

We had to help with the mowing and maintenance, chores like that. There was a lot of mowing to do, and it took a lot of time. We had a tractor, but that didn't work for everything. I did like to run the equipment, especially that tractor. I'd ride around with Dad while he worked on odd jobs at the campground and spend that time with him. Watching Dad helped teach me how to take responsibility for other things when I grew up. I learned the value of work, too.

The campground had a swimming pond and a pond for fishing. We had paddle boats on the pond, too. It was great. We didn't have a swimming pool, just the pond for swimming, but a lot of people liked that better. You could go in the water with inner tubes and other paraphernalia, which you can't do in a regular pool. But then things changed a little with concerns about safety, and people wanted the swimming pool.

There was a time when my parents had a six-wheeler ATV that people could take out on the pond. I remember one time when my dad ran out of gas out there, and we had to throw him a fishing line and pull him back in.

The campground had a store in case anyone needed supplies. Mother ran the store. We did take turns taking her place in the store when it was really hot. The store did not have any air conditioning, so then we'd take turns in the pond. Tim helped more with the store while I helped my dad more with maintenance and repairs.

Mom liked the time after the store closed at night. We'd have campfires and sit around and talk. She'd make s'mores and we'd have Moon Pies. It was our time to relax after the day. The campground was just down the hill from the family home, about thirty feet away. When we were done for the night, we could get away a little bit.

When Grandfather Harvey, my grandfather on my mother's side, used to live there, he would come down and take care of the store. He'd help rake the leaves and do other jobs, too. My brother and I also had to rake the leaves. In fact, we'd get into fights about doing the leaves until one of us would get mad and walk away. I think my grandfather figured that was going to happen. He didn't say a whole lot about it.

My parents made the campground family-oriented, and they always tried to keep it that way. They wanted the campers to feel like family. The fun part was getting to know all these people you'd never meet otherwise. A lot of them felt like family because you'd see them so often. Some of the seasonal people were with us so long that when they finally passed away, it was like losing a family member.

I met people from all over and built some friendships along the way. My most vivid memory was how my brother created a club and how our friends from the campground were all in it. We did imaginary things like playing Cowboys and Indians. We had the Matchbox cars, and we set them up and made roads and such like.

My parents had family activities for the campers. My mom came up with most of the ideas; she was very creative. She liked to be around people, so that was a big part of it, too. For instance, my parents would have a fishing competition at the campground, to see who could get the biggest fish. They'd have trophies for it.

They also offered bingo and had me calling the numbers. People were on pins and needles waiting for those numbers! Bingo was every weekend, so I didn't always want to do it, but it was fun.

Another activity they provided were Frisbee golf tournaments, where you'd use Frisbees in place of the balls and have to throw them over the holes. People still love that; they have it at the campground even now. It's a big thing for some people. The course was set up by a college professor my dad knew from when he went to college. This friend was really into it. He went to big competitions and knew what he was doing.

We used to have chicken barbecues, as well. There was a deck around the store with picnic tables, and everybody would come up and have a get-together. There were potluck dinners where everybody brought different dishes. You got to try a lot of different food, and that's where my mom got a lot of different recipes, like the one for shoofly pie, which Tim really liked. There's a wet and a dry version. I've never been able to figure out the difference, but I think Mom made the dry one.

Tim is a little better at baking than I am. He worked with my mother on that because he was interested back then. Nowadays, when he and his wife come to family dinners, he's always the one who makes the food they bring. I wish now I'd paid a little more attention like he did back then.

Mom organized a scavenger hunt at the campground and had candy scrambles for the kids during Labor Day weekend for the last weekend the camp was open. That was later on, when my parents started to close earlier for the year.

Before that change, we'd have Halloween parties where we'd stay up late. People would decorate, and they'd have a parade where kids could decorate their bicycles and parade them around the campground.

Mom let Tim and me ride in that, but we couldn't get any prizes. I understand now why she did that, but I didn't always back then.

On Sundays my parents would get somebody to have a church service at the campground. It helped them out, too, because they obviously couldn't get to church on Sunday mornings. This way they still got to enjoy a service. Later on, they arranged for the state park chaplain to come over and do those services.

Once the campground shut down for the season, my parents would take us someplace that we couldn't go when the camp was open. All the weekends were tied up over the summer, so there wasn't time to do much. During the week, you had to get ready to do the next weekend. So, in the fall, we'd just load the back of the pickup truck and go camping ourselves.

It's funny, when you're writing down memories, how you keep coming up with little things that you haven't thought of in years.

It feels good to remember those things.

The Struggle with School

Every fall we were ready to close down the campground, since by then we were ready for that break and starting to get tired.

However, going back to school wasn't my favorite part. Everybody who knows me now will tell you I'm a positive person, but through most of school, I wasn't that positive. Having people who loved and supported me kept me going during that time.

First, I went to Newville Elementary, then it was to Big Spring Middle School up to sixth grade, and finally to Big Spring High School. They put seventh through twelfth grade in the high school. Our school colors were maroon, and gold and our mascot was the bulldog. Go, Big Spring Bulldogs!

I have a lot of the same school memories as everyone else. When cafeteria had pudding or gelatin in the cafeteria, you could turn the bowl upside down, and the pudding or gelatin wouldn't come out, it was that solid. For picture day, we had to wear a decent shirt, but Mother never made us wear a tie. Sometimes those high turtlenecks—I always hated those—felt like they choked you!

I had to go by school bus. It took about a half hour or more to pick up all the students. I remember a couple of times the bus breaking down, too, with all the kids on it. I always liked it if the bus broke down on the way to school—but not on the way home!

Back then, the parents would come looking to see where the bus was and then just pick up all the kids and take them in. They were allowed to do that then. I don't think they could do that today. Back then we knew the whole neighborhood. And if you didn't know them, they knew who your parents were, so if you got in some trouble, your parents would know.

One of the things to remember in country life is that most of your neighbors went to the same church, and that's how you got to know all of them. You knew where you were going to go every Sunday, and you had that fellowship with your family and your neighbors. In the country, you're not that close, and the church was where you did all the talking.

When I got older, I got more sensitive about school. I couldn't do a lot of the things other kids could do, and that was hard for me. Mother was always there for me. I would come home and share with her. She would say to keep a positive attitude and that she believed I could do those things. When I was in fourth grade, someone came to help tutor me at home with math. Mother arranged for that.

I wanted to come home every day. I wanted to be out of school. I didn't have many friends. At that young age, you don't really understand those things. But, at the end of the day, I knew when I came through the door that Mom was going to be there. It was a really good feeling to know that. She was always supportive of me, always taught me to think positive, and constantly pushed me to do better. Even though I went through all those hard things, she just pushed me to keep going.

But I wasn't always positive like that. The reason goes back to the way I was treated by kids. I got a lot of bullying. As a result, I closed in on myself and didn't talk to anybody.

The bullying started about middle school, during the teenage years. Elementary is usually good, but as soon as you get to middle school, everything changes. When you're in elementary, everybody is friends with each other, but when you get to middle school, things are different. Back then I didn't have the physical issues as badly as I do now, but I always had trouble walking and got picked on about it.

I didn't know what was going on with my body, and the doctor was always telling my mother that there was nothing they could do about it.

Gym class was one of the main places where the bullying happened. I couldn't get around like the other kids or do things like they could, and they didn't understand that. They would always pick on the ones who were weak. For me, the problem was my legs. I couldn't run fast like the other kids could around the track. I usually ended up walking half of it. Of course, the gym teacher didn't understand that, either. The teacher always wanted you to run and not walk.

There was one main bully, let's call him Henry. He was the one who would actually hit me. It was part of Henry's routine every day. There were four or five boys in the group, but the others were usually mostly laughing. First, they did the name calling, and they'd get other people involved with it. Other kids would rally with them and chime in.

They used the word *retarded*, a horrible, hurtful word.

Then they got physical. They would start to pinch me, real hard, under the arms, for example. It was the kind of pinch where they'd twist, and it really hurt. The bullying would go on in between classes. There was name calling and hitting, although Henry made sure there were no marks.

Henry would hit me with an open hand mostly, so nobody could see the marks. And if the marks were visible, I'd hide them from my parents. He'd hit me in the back so other people couldn't see if there were marks.

He would catch me in the hallway or the locker area. Or he'd start in on me if the teacher would walk out of the room for a moment. With all the commotion in a hallway or a classroom with no teacher, things like that could happen really quickly. I think some of the teachers saw what was going on, but they never said anything.

I guess they didn't know how to handle it.

I wasn't brave enough to tell anybody. Besides, if kids would tell on the bullies, the bullying could just end up being worse.

Once, I tried to fight back and throw some punches, but I ended up losing my balance on the floor, so it didn't look so good.

I did have one friend; our friendship went back to middle school. But I think he was afraid that these things would end up happening to him, too. One day, he just stopped being my friend.

When he didn't stick up for me, it made me feel like he wasn't a real friend. A real friend would stand up for you. I think now he was intimidated and afraid. But back then, I never saw it that way.

I didn't tell anyone about all of this. In my mind, I was ashamed. I know it wasn't my fault, but it felt like it.

The bullying was awful. It makes you question yourself sometimes.

I never told my parents about the physical part. I don't know why.

Mother probably knew but just didn't say anything. She could pick up on when I had a really hard day. She told me that she loved and supported me and that she was there for me. I felt a lot better when I got home. She was great at giving hugs.

But then it was time to go back to school again.

I didn't want to go, but she pushed me to go back. After all, I knew I didn't have a choice. You had to go back to school the next day. And I'm glad I did. I didn't want to disappoint my parents. I wanted to graduate from school and do better for myself. So, I kept going back. It wasn't easy, but I did it.

Well, most of the time, I did.

I started to make excuses to try and not go to school. I'd say I was sick, that my stomach was hurting, things like that. It wasn't that I didn't want to learn; I just didn't want to face those bullies. In those days we had to wear a gym outfit to participate in gym class, so I started conveniently forgetting my gym clothes. We never really talked about it, but because I was trying to get out of school every week, I think Mom finally caught on to that excuse.

I wanted to learn, but the things that went on in school made me feel down every day, so I probably didn't do the work like I should have.

In the cafeteria, you had to find your own place to sit. Nobody would let you sit with them, so you had to find your own table. When I sat there, eating my lunch by myself, I just felt all alone, like I never was going to have any friends.

Sometimes I would have the same lunch period with my brother, and he would usually let me sit with his friends. That felt pretty good.

Childhood, Christmas and the Campground

Back then, it was mostly my brother who was my friend. I don't know if Tim knew about the bullying. He had to have, but he never said much.

I wasn't doing well in my classes, and I wasn't fitting in. The teachers thought I had a learning disability, so in seventh grade they put me in a smaller class. But my mother had me pulled right out of that because she knew that wasn't my problem. Back then, school officials just tried to place anybody with any kind of disability that way. I probably never would have learned anything if I'd stayed there.

The bullying went on until I started high school. It did get better when Henry finally moved away. I remember celebrating that day. After he was gone, the bullying was more verbal, like threats that they were "gonna beat you up," but it never got that far. These bullies would pick on you if you sat toward the back of the bus, so I always sat near the front.

But even after this boy moved away, the scars were still there ... for a long time.

One thing that helped me was taking a Vo-Ag (Vocational Agriculture) class. As part of the Future Farmers of America (FFA) program, each one of us got to raise an animal by ourselves. I worked with a cow that was about to have a calf. She was the kind of cow that would just let me come up and pet her. She liked that. I helped raise the calf, which was special.

The teacher, my favorite one ever, was Miss Betsy Merchant. She supported and encouraged me and told me that I could do things I thought I couldn't. She had faith in me. I made some friends in FFA. We had our own little group and kind of stuck up for each other. When we went to lunch, we'd eat together and hang out. That's when I finally felt good about going to school.

When I started having a hard time with other things in school, I realized that going to church helped. I realized that God was the One who was there for me. Miss Merchant talked me into being the chaplain for some FFA meetings, and I held that position for two years.

One year, to support the local farmers, I volunteered to be part of a presentation at the local mall. We dressed up in cow costumes. Otherwise, I wasn't involved in any extracurricular activities. Eventually, Miss Merchant got married and moved away, and that was sad.

I went to some of the football games with a few of my friends in Vo-Ag. There was a traditional rivalry game between Shippensburg High School and Big Spring High School. They had this little brown jug, and whichever school's team won, that school got the jug for the year. The "Little Brown Jug" game still goes on today.

When I first turned sixteen and could drive to that first FFA meeting, that was great. That's when I became popular—because I was the first one who could drive.

But I never went to any dances or celebrations at school. I never got to experience any of that.

Thinking back on the 1970s when I grew up, I did enjoy my life. I did like learning new things. I remember when we switched from a black and white TV to color TV. That was an experience! There was a convenience store in Newville that had pinball machines, which was the popular hangout. There wasn't a curfew in town, but my parents didn't like us to stay out late. We'd go to bed at a certain time every night, so that was my curfew.

I think a lot of things are easier now, like having GPS in the car so you don't need to read a map to know where you're going. Once Debbie and I got one of those, I was happy! It always seemed like you had a good direction mapped out, but the route went wrong one way or another. I also like how you can look everybody up in your contacts

Childhood, Christmas and the Campground

without a phone book. Before, you memorized the numbers; now you just look them up. It would be pretty horrible to be without the contacts list and have to remember.

My dad had to go back to school just like us because he was a teacher, and he didn't look forward to going back either, sometimes. He taught sixth grade, back at a time when they still respected the teachers. Then things changed. That's why he retired early. It got to the point where the kids didn't have that respect anymore, and you had to watch what you did because you could get in trouble very easily. My dad gave teaching his best as long as he could. I think he probably had a sense of humor in his classroom. The kids really seemed to like him.

I graduated in 1985. It was a tough year. Mom was fighting cancer and Grandfather Sheldon died. He passed in the fall, the year I graduated. He'd been like a best friend to me. Our time together was special, but I never told him about my hard times at school.

I had an English teacher in twelfth grade who really encouraged me, too: Jill Davis. She was the kind of teacher whom everybody liked. She had lots of energy. Even a couple of years after you graduated, she'd always say "hi" to you every time she saw you. I needed all the encouragement I could get that year!

My mother attended my graduation, which was a special thing because that was right after her time dealing with cancer. She always told me I could do what I needed to and wouldn't let me think negatively. It was the same with my dad. I wanted to make my parents proud by graduating.

And I did.

My family, the campground, the farm, my church family—all played a part in getting me to where I am today. It took a while to get there, but I'm here!

CHAPTER TWO
Something Missing, Something Found

Grown-Up

After graduation, I lived at home with my parents. We were able to take some longer trips. Our parents took me and Tim out West to see Yellowstone and then the Grand Canyon. They had a motor home, and they let the two of us take it over to the state park and camp together, too. When I lived at home, if I wanted to go to the movies with them, they'd bring me along. I remember one time we all went to see the movie *Gettysburg*. During that time, when I lived at home, Mom got a chance to substitute and teach some music again. That brought her a lot of joy.

Even after I was eighteen, my parents still never let us get out of going to church. As long as we were under their roof, going to church was not negotiable, and that was good for us.

As a grown-up, I needed a job. I heard about an opening at Pine Grove Furnace State Park through the state and applied. It's a wonderful park, with 696 acres at the Northern Tip of the Blue Ridge Mountains, in an area they call South Mountain. It's confusing, I know! The park had walking trails, a lake you could swim in, and a lake you could fish in, along with paddle boats and other equipment. They also had bicycle trails. Later in life, I did some bicycling on those trails myself.

It was the kind of position for people first starting out. In fact, it was part of a program to help young people get started with work. The park was redoing the office building at the time. We got to knock all the plaster walls down. I remember being covered with white dust by the time I got home. I was exhausted! Then we helped to put up the dry wall and install the counters when it was rebuilt. People still use that building today to check in when they go camping there.

We also built two pavilions that are still there today. The park still has signs telling everybody it was our crew that worked on the pavilions.

My first boss was pretty good. It was my first time working away from home, and I learned the meaning of working under somebody. It can be challenging, learning to follow directions, but that's a very good asset.

Later, I worked at an auto parts store where I drove parts around to the different garages. It was one of those really good jobs where the pay wasn't the greatest. I loved it, though. I always liked cars and was into parts. I really understood them. I liked the driving part as well; I always liked to drive.

The manager, John, invited me and some other people who worked with us to go out on his boat. He had just bought the boat not long before. He wanted me to try water-skiing, too. I never got up on the water skis, but I tried! They had a tube I could hold onto, and that was fun. That outing was the first experience I ever had on the river, so it was a little scary!

The employees started a bowling league when I was working there as well. We did that for a while. I enjoyed it. The spirit was nice. It wasn't all about winning or losing. Everyone had fun either way.

That was one of my favorite jobs I had. It also got me into pursuing diesel mechanics. Having been around diesel engines on that job, I wanted to learn to work on the diesel engines in trucks, buses and large construction equipment.

There was an Open House for a two-year program at Williamsport Community College, and my mother encouraged me to go. So, I quit the driving job and went to school for diesel mechanics. By the time I graduated, the community college had become part of Penn State.

As part of my schooling, I was taking some truck driving courses (you need to be able to test drive the vehicles you're working on). But with the problems I had with my left knee, I couldn't handle the clutch. What happened was—and this was a really scary moment—I was driving down this hill and couldn't get the clutch back in. So, the truck was coasting downhill and picking up speed. The instructor kept me calm and helped me slow it down. He said if we slam on the brakes, we will jack-knife. Fortunately, he stayed calm. He had to be calm because he knew that, otherwise, I would panic.

The instructor then recommended I undergo knee surgery. He'd been in a truck accident a few years before, and he said it really helped him do normal movements again when he got that surgery.

I talked to my parents about it first, then we went to a doctor and got x-rays. For a while, my doctor didn't want to do the surgery because he wasn't sure if it would work or not. But my mom and I talked to him and finally convinced him to do it. The doctor wanted to be truthful and make sure we knew that it might not work. Still, I wanted to try and see if it would help.

It was supposed to be outpatient surgery, and it took four or five hours. I was a little bit scared. I was still living at home then, so my parents were there for me. My mother said she loved me before I went in for the operation. That meant a lot.

My parents were there when I woke up in recovery. I was in a lot of pain, and the doctors decided it was best that I stay overnight.

The next day, when I left the hospital, there was a snowstorm, so my parents couldn't come in to pick me up. The staff drove me home in this ambulance, but I could feel the back sliding like it was coming off the road.

I had rehab, and there were snowstorms in the middle of that, too. Some days I couldn't get there. I was impatient because I wanted to get to the appointments and get walking again. But sometimes it wasn't safe enough to go. There was my impatience again.

My parents had a small Chevy Cavalier, but since my leg had to be straight, I couldn't get in that car. I had to go in their pickup.

The rehabilitation was painful. The therapists put weights on to try and get my leg straightened back up. I ended up opting out on the painkillers because I couldn't function on the medicine they were giving me. Mom noticed that. They said, "Try Tylenol," and it was hard to do that, too. I endured a lot more pain as a result. One day the therapists put me on a new machine, and I passed out. They had to take me off that and put me on the mat. I think it was something about the blood flow.

But I was determined, and I wanted to walk again.

It took almost a year to get the use of my legs back, but I did start walking again. During that time, I needed help to take showers and get dressed. I couldn't do that by myself at that time. It's hard when you're used to being an adult and independent, and then you have to accept help like that.

My mother went through cancer two times. I saw how she fought and kept coming back, and she gave me that fight.

In the end, the surgery helped with my walking, but I never was able to get the leg strength to be able to use the clutch.

That inability discouraged me because, at that time, I was working toward doing the mechanic part of the schoolwork and working toward getting the State Inspections License. But you can't get that if you can't drive the truck.

That was my dream. I really wanted to do that. It was one of those things I got to try, and it never worked out. At least I did get to experience it a little.

Through all of that, I got laid off. I was off too much, and they couldn't understand that. I had been working eight-hour days, even longer than that sometimes because you couldn't always anticipate when the trucks would come in.

After I was back on my feet again, I ended up working at a Sheetz convenience store in Mechanicsburg, a larger town about an hour away from home. At first, I tried the cashier position, and that didn't go real well. Then they offered me a position doing the stocking, and that worked out. I asked if they would pay the wage that the cashier got, and they agreed to that.

I'd restock the milk and the soda, and then, since I was in charge of the parking lot, I'd make sure that was clean. I took care of the garbage outside and all that outdoor paraphernalia. When it snowed, I had to run the snowblower. But at least they had one of those!

One year there was a big snowstorm, and they had to put me up in a motel for a whole week because I couldn't get home!

There's a Sheetz store in Newville now, which is about ten minutes away from my home, but back then only a couple of the stores were in the area. At that time, it was a long drive for gas in Newville. My parents, however, had a tank that they'd get filled and had their gas that way. After all, they had the tractors to run and so they had to have gas around.

I worked there for about five years, or something like that. The Sheetz is still there. They tore down the old building and rebuilt everything again because it was getting outdated. Sheetz does that every few years and updates all the stores.

Even the things that stay the same have a way of changing.

Debbie

I was about thirty years old and still living at home. Mom wanted me to go out and meet somebody so I wouldn't be by myself. She got me out there.

The idea had been on my mind. Tim had gotten married a few years before to Connie, who's still his wife today. He'd gone to study at the seminary in Columbus, Ohio, and was ordained as a minister at our family church, St. Peter's in Newville. He and Connie went back to Columbus, where he had his first church. Today, Connie is also a pastor at a Lutheran church in York, Pennsylvania.

I was the best man at their wedding, and that's when I realized I wanted to find somebody I could spend the rest of my life with. I wanted it when I saw all the love between Tim and Connie that day.

So, I joined the New Genesis Singles Ministry in Carlisle. It was a church group for singles where the members got together to meet each other. It would start as a friend thing, and then you'd get to know each other.

I had a hard time finding people, so a lady named Deb Rutz invited me to sit at her table with her group. We started out that way with a friendship, just talking. She was about forty years old, ten years older than me, with an outgoing personality. We talked about family. She had three brothers. Debbie was the second-oldest child. Barry was her older brother; Doug was younger; and then Don was the youngest.

Don was her favorite brother. At first, as a little girl, she wasn't keen on his arrival. She told me that she had wanted a sister. Debbie locked herself in the bathroom, and her father had to come get her out because she was so mad. She already had two brothers, who needs a third? But then, he ended up being her favorite, so it worked out.

Give things a chance, and you never know what will happen.

Deb asked me to go to the movies. I went with two girls, Debbie and her friend Pam. They told me later that they were kind of guessing which one I was going to pick. Pam would share rides when we went to events and such. We were just friends then. Deb was always fun to be with, and I didn't know at the time that it was going to become more than that.

I just knew that we had a lot in common. She had a really good sense of humor, and we had a lot of the same interests. Deb loved animals and nature as much as I did. We were both Christians and believed in the church and believed in family. That was really important.

Each year, New Genesis would invite everyone to go to the shore. It ended up being a lot of people's vacations at that time. Our trip was to Ocean City, Maryland. I'd say about twelve people were there. The men shared rooms with other men and the women with women. So, Debbie and I were on the trip together, but also separate.

However, that's when things came together. We kind of had two matchmakers. These two friends would walk down the beach with me, saying things like, "Do you like her?" I didn't realize then what they were doing, but it didn't hurt. I still talk to one of those friends on Facebook. She says she still remembers how Debbie and I had that special relationship.

I was lying out in the sun on a towel, with no umbrella. Debbie said, "You can come under my umbrella with me on my towel." And we fell asleep. One of our friends came and took a picture of us sleeping on the towel. Neither of us knew about it until the picture got developed. I still have it somewhere.

Debbie liked to watch the boats; I liked to do that, too. We also watched the people at the shore. And when we got home, she asked me out.

It was my very first date.

The first time we went out, we went on a hayride. It was a "haunted hayride" for Halloween, just the two of us together. It was a great idea, since we could use it as an excuse to get close, too. We got scared, so we ended up hugging, holding each other tight. That first night, we hugged each other before she got out of the car and talked about going out again. That time I made the call to ask her out, and we went to a movie.

After that, there was no stopping us. She was my first love.

I remember how our favorite song that we would dance to while we were dating was "Lady in Red" by Chris de Burgh:

> *The lady in red*
> *Is dancing with me*
> *Cheek to cheek,*
> *There's nobody here,*
> *It's just you and me,*
> *It's where I want to be*[3]

Debbie really brought me around to the positive. I think I lived at home so long because those bad feelings from school still lingered. She gave me a new way of seeing things. That's when I started to be able to make friends, too; she would make friends with people, then they would be stuck and would be our friends after that.

Those friends are still there for me now.

I had been Lutheran, but I ended up going to Deb's church, the First United Church of Christ (UCC) in Carlisle. The service was pretty much the same, since the UCC has strong Lutheran roots. We went with Debbie's whole family, and I got to know her family that way. My mom and dad were okay with that. They understood.

Even before I became a member of the church, one of Debbie's friends asked me to join their choir. It was very special to have her hear me singing there. It was important to her that we met through the church because she really believed in her faith, and that was something I was looking for, too.

We got married on April 19, 1997.

After I decided to propose, it took me a whole month before I actually got the courage to follow through. I took Debbie out, meaning to pop the question, but I got nervous and the food was late, which messed the whole thing up. But once I did propose and she said "yes," we went together and picked out the rings. I remember we went to a couple of different places to shop around.

---

3 Chris de Burgh, "Lady in Red," Album *Into the Light*, Copyright 1986, A&M Records Ltd.

Since I really liked Debbie's church, I decided we should have the wedding there. I became a member at that church a couple of months after we were married. Lynn Schultz and Wanda Veldmen, the main and associate pastors, officiated.

The biggest thing I can remember is when Debbie first walked down the aisle and I started crying because I was so happy.

> *I'll never forget*
> *The way you look tonight*[4]

Our wedding day was a sunny day, but very chilly—one of those cold spring days. We had purple flowers. I can't remember what they were, but purple was her favorite color. I left picking the flowers to her. Our four brothers were my groomsmen. Tim was my best man. Debbie had a good friend from work who was the bridesmaid. The pastor, Lynn Schultz, would always kid us that we had the longest kiss he'd ever seen after he said, "You may kiss the bride."

---

4 Ibid.

Something Missing, Something Found

We went to the Poconos for our honeymoon. My parents went there for theirs, and they recommended it. I remember the heart-shaped hot tub in our suite and the big three-course meal they offered every night. It was all very romantic.

From that day forward, we were Mr. and Mrs. Mentzer.
Till death do us part.

The Happiest Years of Our Lives
We didn't even know if we were going to have a house at first. The original plan was for us to move into the old house that my grandmother had lived in, but there was too much work to fix it up to do that.

We all went and looked at a used double-wide a couple of miles down the road from us. My mother saw an ad in the paper. It was what we wanted, so we bought it. My parents offered us the property to put it on, and a couple of weeks before we got married, Debbie and I had a place to live.

Being nearby, we could help with the campground. That was the deal. However, it could be good and bad to live that close to your parents. They would always know what you were doing. You couldn't sneak a day off work since they would know! You also couldn't say, "Oh, we can't make it today," or "We're too sick for work today," since they'd be over checking on you. As for my parents, they could simply step outside and see what was going on with us! They would get concerned because sometimes I would stay late after work and they wanted to make sure I was okay with the car. It was Mom's way of caring, but it could get to be a little much. At the time we didn't realize how much she did to help me. I didn't always like it, but when I look back, I can see it.

I appreciated that help when Mom would bring meals over for a few days when Debbie came home from the hospital and rested until she was ready to start doing things again. They would come meet me at the hospital, too, when Debbie was having some physical troubles.

Deb was a nurse's aide who took care of patients and did all the administration, too. She worked at Carlisle Hospital for thirty years. A caring person by nature, she put herself out there caring for her patients. A lot of those people would remember her after their surgeries. We'd run into them out in public, and they'd thank her for the care she gave to them.

Debbie would tell me stories from the hospital, from stories about the patients she helped to the story about the doctor who was in the bathroom and didn't lock the door, so she walked in on him. It was a fast-paced, high-stress job, and there was always something going on.

Debbie liked to go to the movies. That was her favorite thing in life. We went to the theaters a lot for a while and shared the popcorn. Friday nights after work, we'd have our date night at the movies. I can't do horror, though. I would start dreaming about all that bad stuff at night, and I could not handle that. My wife talked me into seeing *Scream*. That was bad! Payback for the hayride! She liked them, though. But her favorite type was the action movie.

Deb liked to watch TV as well, so I'd watch more with her, but when I'm by myself, I'm more of an outside person. My wife had lived in town and always had cable. I didn't have that out in the country, so it didn't make much difference to me. However, she wanted it, and when we got it, then Mom wanted it, too, instead of the satellite dish she'd had before. I like having cable in the winter when there's more sports on that I can watch.

Debbie liked to watch Westerns on TV. I always remember how, on those cold, ugly days, my wife and I would watch Westerns together and pop popcorn or snuggle in bed late at night and keep each other warm and talk. We didn't watch things separately.

When you look back, you see how fast the time goes. It was good that we had all that quality time together.

We even did the laundry together. Our marriage was a partnership. I first started helping with the laundry when Debbie was working and wouldn't get home till later. That was something I could take care of. My mother kind of started that. She said, "You do realize that she works late. You could do the laundry." Mom just slid it in there. I think she realized that she was home all the time and did the laundry, so she just wanted to put that out there, that I could help.

The job I had was regular hours, but with Debbie often working late, I was home a little more where I could do those things. It helped me not to think "where was she at" and all that. It also helped later when I needed to take care of her, and I already knew how to do those kinds of household chores.

What I was really proud of was installing the kitchen sink. My wife was a little apprehensive about me doing it by myself, but it all worked out.

Cooking wasn't her favorite thing, but Deb still liked to do it. More of a baker, she made great angel food cake, and I really liked that. I especially miss her scalloped pineapple. Everybody loved that dish. Debbie made brownies for me, and there was this Parmesan chicken dish that I liked. She also enjoyed making cookies at Christmastime.

Christmas was my favorite time with Debbie. She really loved the Christmas tree and all the decorations. Our tradition was to turn off all the house lights and just leave on the Christmas tree lights. We had a small living room, so when the tree lights were on, they lit up the whole house. It was a nice, quiet, romantic moment then. I still did that on my own last year, but I really miss the quiet time with Debbie.

During some of the holidays, we'd spend time with her family, then come home and spend time with my parents. Usually we were tired by the time we got to the second place, but it's something you have to do. My brother lived in Ohio, so he'd come up after Christmas. We'd exchange gifts then, and eventually we just started doing it that way.

Deb always loved it when birthdays and anniversaries came around. My birthday is April 17 (right before our anniversary), while hers was January 29. I would take her somewhere special to eat out. She liked the Olive Garden and Applebee's restaurants. On Sundays after church, we always went out to eat with her family. We both enjoyed that very much. Some of our favorite places to go with them were Cracker Barrel, the Fairground Diner and Walnut Bottom Diner, the latter two both being in Carlisle.

When I drove to see my doctor in Hershey on Wednesdays, Debbie and I would make a day of it, checking out Hersheypark and watching the people ride the roller coasters. I'm really going to miss that.

We went to Pigeon Forge, a resort city in Tennessee, with Debbie's brothers and mother for our first big trip. That's the farthest we ever went. Her family had one of those timeshare contracts where they can take vacations and bring people with them. We took our car and drove the whole way—a ten-hour drive. You have to leave early in the morning, but you can make it in one day. We got to see everything along the way, and Debbie and I both loved the Pigeon Forge area. I remember we saw Louise Mandrell in concert and toured the Smokey Mountains while we were there. We really liked that.

Another memorable trip my wife and I took was to Niagara Falls. There is this boat, the Maid of the Mist, which takes people beneath the waterfalls. We signed up for the tour package, so we got to see most everything, including the sights on the Canadian side, too. We had so much fun!

Oftentimes we would simply get in the car and take car rides, just exploring different areas. We always liked to look at the different houses around and dream about the ones we really loved. Debbie liked the wraparound porches; she always liked to look at the bigger houses. I miss how, when we went by this one barn in Bloserville, Debbie always counted how many horses were in the barn.

Once we went to Virginia—before we had GPS—and the map made it look like a direct route. Instead, it was uphill and downhill and all over the place. We went the "scenic route" for a couple of hours!

One time we went to the Knoebels Amusement Park in Elysburg, Pennsylvania. They had bumper boats there. We were out in the middle of the water when Debbie's boat ran out of gas. I was looking around for her and finally saw her motioning around looking for somebody to come out and put gas in the boat. We laughed about that for years.

She showed me how to never give up on anything. Debbie was strong in her faith, and she went through a rough divorce before she married me. I saw that she got through that. However, it really scarred her, too; there were some things she couldn't remember about her childhood because of that inner scarring. I didn't know all of that at the time; some of it came out later talking to her brother Barry. Debbie would never talk much about that.

I know it meant a lot to her to become part of my family. My parents considered Debbie to be a daughter, not just my wife. Dad really liked Debbie. Early in our marriage, she had lost her own father, and my dad became like the father she didn't have anymore. There were times when I was working and couldn't be with Debbie when she had anxiety, and Mom and Dad would stay with her or take her with them and do things together.

One time when I wasn't there, Debbie had a mild stroke. That scared her, so she didn't want to stay at the house alone. Mother went to the doctor with her and told him that he needed to get her some help.

Since I was still working then, my parents would pick her up and take her places to get her out of the house.

My wife would invite both my mother and her mother to mother-daughter banquets at the church. She really enjoyed that. Mom didn't have a daughter, so it was special for her, too, that she still got to go to a mother-daughter banquet. Because we lived so close to my parents, there was that family connection.

No matter what kind of problems Debbie was having, she was always able to get herself together to help when my mother was in the hospital. Debbie was a helper. She was there for her brothers, for me and for my parents, always helping out the best way she knew how.

One day, after we'd been married for about a year, my right knee gave out on me as I was coming out of the shower, much the same way my left knee had years before. I had a bad fall. My foot bent back, too, but luckily didn't break. My wife literally had to pick me up because I couldn't get up on that leg.

We went to the emergency room, and the staff did x-rays and wrapped it. Then they told me I had to go to the doctor and have it looked at. I didn't really want to go, but I knew I needed to. Debbie wanted to call the ambulance, but I was determined that she wouldn't need to do that. There was pride involved, as well as the cost of riding in the ambulance. My left leg was still doing pretty well; I had to put most of my weight on that one with the right knee giving out.

The doctor said it was a meniscus tear and that I had to have it removed. In short, I needed another operation. My wife was there for me. She told me to keep going. Deb worked at a unit close to where I got my surgery, so she got to sneak in and see me beforehand. Well, she didn't "sneak" in; rather, they let her in, but she maybe wasn't supposed to be there.

She told me that she loved me. That was what I needed.

When I woke up, I remember seeing my wife. This was outpatient surgery, and I just wanted to leave. I remember needing to throw up, but when they asked me if I was sick, I said I wasn't and held it back so I could get out of there. Debbie wasn't too happy with that, since I threw up when we got to the car. But I just wanted to leave! However, I don't know that she appreciated being there that time!

I sat in my recliner while I recovered, since they wanted me to keep my knee upright. They told me to walk on it lightly. I did some home exercises to rehabilitate it. I was still working at Sheetz then and wasn't able to go back to work for about two months. I couldn't put weight on the knee and was using a cane or walker to get around.

There was leave I could use, but I ran out of leave. Toward the end of my recuperation, my insurance ran out, and I ended up going on COBRA. (If you're not familiar with that, it's from The Consolidated Omnibus Budget Reconciliation Act of 1985, which lets workers continue their health insurance from work for a short period if it runs out.)

I think the biggest fear I had then was that I knew this injury would keep me off work for a while and we needed that income. But we had each other, and that was the important part. It doesn't make the time easy, but knowing we have each other takes some of the heaviness away.

The local food bank helped us out. I remember waiting in those lines to get food. That was tough. But we did meet some nice people along the way who talked to us. You meet some of the kindest people in places like that. The hardest part was that some of the people volunteering there knew me, too. That was a lot to deal with. It wasn't easy to get in that line the first time, but when we pray and ask for help, we have to take that help when it's provided.

Sometimes we would go back to St. Peter's for a special service, like their Homecoming Service. We'd become a big part of the UCC by then. The church helped us out with the bills, such as the electric bill, at that time, too. To have times like that early on in our marriage was hard, but we got through it together. My parents helped us out as well.

It was about six months or so before I went back to work. Management decided they weren't going to give me full-time, just half-days. But that ended up working out, too, in a way, because by then Debbie needed to have a hysterectomy. I was glad I was able to help her out with the extra time I had.

I know that surgery was hard for her. But I kept being there and supporting her and giving her big hugs whenever I could. It's the little things that really matter. I just remember, when I would kiss her, those loving eyes. I always knew how she felt.

The doctor wanted me to have half-days at first when I went back to work at Sheetz. The walking was getting better. I still had some pain, but it wasn't nearly what it had been, and I was pretty much off the cane and walker by then. The goal was to get the strength back to do the things I needed to again.

After our circumstances got straightened out, I went for a different job to work full-time again. That felt pretty good. First, I got a job with vehicle parts again. But I was only at that job for about a week. It didn't work out.

Then I went to work at the Newville Ribbon Company, and that was great because it wasn't far away. I had a ten-minute drive and I was there. My job was to wind ribbons on spools. The ribbon was the backing for women's bras; the spools then got sent off to the factory where the bras were made. The material was heavy; you'd have to tape up your fingers so they wouldn't get cut. I was able to get a full forty hours there, and things were looking up again.

Debbie and I were cat people. When we lost our previous cat, we decided around Christmas in 2015 that we would get a new one as our Christmas present to each other.

A friend drove us about two hours to a rescue place where this foster family had a whole bunch of cats they were taking care of. When someone would come in who was interested, that person would adopt a cat out from there.

The cat we picked out was Sweetie. She was a short-haired cat (I'm not sure about the breed) who's been very good company ever since, a real friendly cat. Her name was Olive originally, but since we didn't care for that name, we changed it. She didn't really answer to Olive anyway, so I don't think she liked it either.

Sweetie had a hard life before we got her, but we got her straightened out. She was overweight, so much so that when we first got her, we couldn't even pick her up. But eventually we got her down to her normal healthy weight, and she's been in good shape ever since.

I remember that Sweetie didn't really care for that ride back. We had to stop every couple of minutes after she threw up to clean up everything.

In our marriage, Debbie and I never lost the love. We were really close the whole time. It never changed from where we started. We always liked to hold hands. On cold, freezing winter mornings, we liked to snuggle and talk to each other. We'd talk about how fast the years went by, still feeling that love and closeness for each other.

I'll always miss how Deb would look at me when she wanted a kiss, with those bright, loving eyes. I'll miss her laughter and her sense of humor—the little things. I'll miss how she always was telling me I missed a spot when I was shaving. To this day, I never miss that spot. I'll miss the way she didn't like it when I wore too much blue: "You've got other colored clothes, too!" I miss it all.

Struggles and Blessings
Deb's brother Doug passed away from leukemia in 1999. He was only in his forties. She really had a tough time with that. Doug was her younger brother, the stronger one whom you never thought you'd have to worry about. I did my best to support her, and she leaned on her faith.

Doug's wife had called for everyone to come down and see him one last time. We were with Don and Linda when the call came, so we all drove down together, about an hour's drive to Harrisburg. We were able to all be there when he passed.

Doug loved football and coached all three of his sons. He was always there for them. I remember seeing all three of his sons at the funeral, along with all the families and kids he'd touched as a coach. It was wonderful for Debbie to see all that support.

I'd always had trouble walking. In my generation, the doctors didn't really know what was going on. When I was a kid, the medical people said there wasn't anything they could do about it. I'd be walking and then, all of a sudden, just go down.

In 2001, I finally got a diagnosis.

In fact, it was on September 11, 2001.

I remember that I was at the ribbon factory working when 9/11 hit. I remember how everything got quiet when there were no airplanes in the air. We'd always hear them going over the building, but not that day. I remember getting home and just being glad to be home. I had a doctor's appointment that day. Deb knew we were going to get the results, so she got off work early and came with me.

I was diagnosed with muscular dystrophy.

I remember saying that day that I didn't want to be in a wheelchair for the rest of my life. At that point, I was still quite active. Debbie told me that I could do it, that I could walk. I fought that prognosis for as long as I could, and for a long time, I could still walk.

All that positivity and love being poured into me helped to keep me going. I remember my mother having a hard time at first with the diagnosis when she found out. I can understand why. It was tough.

It was frustrating to have physical challenges, but I wasn't the kind of person to give up. I always did fight when things like that happened to me. It was built in me to fight, to keep going.

It was instilled in me by my parents and by my wife—all fighters.

The doctor told me that he'd seen so many people who have what I have just give up. I never think of it as a handicap. Some people think it's terrible to have this life, but it has never stopped me. My mother never wanted me to think that way.

The doctor told me that if I would keep moving, that would keep me going. I did my best to do that. I can say, I fought to walk for as long as I could.

In 2005, Tim and his wife adopted a baby named Andrew, and he became my nephew. His mother wasn't in a very good situation, and she gave him up so he'd have a better life.

We don't think of him as adopted; he's just family. Debbie was the first one who actually got him to laugh and roll over when he was a baby. She loved that moment.

When Andrew was younger, he would come up to my parents' house and all four of us would go out and play baseball with him. (My sister-in-law Connie taught Andrew baseball more than anybody because she used to play.) We also had a four-wheeled ATV that four people could ride in, and we'd go around in that, too.

Another thing I remember is that, with my handicap, Andrew would figure out things I could do with him. He knew there were some things I couldn't do, and he figured that out all on his own. I was his best friend when he came up to visit; he always wanted to do things with me.

The skills and values that my parents shared with me, I can pass along to Andrew. He is sensitive to helping other kids; he's pretty good at that. I like to think he learned some of that from me.

Debbie and I never had children of our own, so we really poured ourselves into having a nephew. We loved shopping for Andrew. I always enjoyed the chance to go toy shopping for him when we could let our inner children out to look at the toys. Debbie and I would play in the store with the ones that made different sounds and did different things just to see what they did.

Easter was a great time with the family. My wife and I and my parents would load up in the Suburban and go to my brother's and enjoy the time with him and his family. They were just starting to have Easter egg hunts with Andrew around that time. We'd bring toys as gifts, maybe a stuffed animal, for Andrew. We'd leave on Friday morning and come back Sunday after the meal. My dad did the driving.

On one trip, my wife decided to give up hamburgers for Lent. We couldn't stop anywhere for hamburgers because she'd made that promise! But she sure was excited to have one on the way back! For Lent, you want to give up something special to you, something you liked. I usually tried to give up chocolate. It didn't always work, but I tried!

When I had to stand at the ribbon factory, my legs would give out after a while from standing all day. But I was still determined to go do my job. Eventually, in 2008 when the economy started to go down, the factory wasn't getting as much business and started to lay people off. They didn't have enough work for everybody. I couldn't always get the work done in a certain time, either, even though I was doing my best, so I was one of the first to go. I went to an OVR (Office of Vocational Rehabilitation) counselor, who recommended trying to go on disability rather than looking for another job at that time.

I was able to get unemployment while I waited for a finding on my disability claim. You have to wait a while for that. There's a lot of paperwork to fill out! It took almost three years to have an official finding, but I was able to get back payments for the period when it was being processed.

During the recession, it was a struggle. We had to make a tank of gas last a whole week. Sometimes it got down near empty before we could afford to fill the tank again. There wasn't much we could do other than live on the basics. But Debbie and I were in it together, trying to make it work. Once again, mom and dad helped us get through this tough time.

It was around this time that I decided I was going to lose weight to try and help keep the pressure off of my legs. That helped with the walking for a while. At that time, my mother was walking for exercise, too, so I'd walk with her, and that was good for both of us. My dad didn't always want to exercise like he should have. I wish he had, for it would have been good for his health. Still, I'm glad I was there to give Mom someone to do it with.

Eventually, my left leg got to the point where I couldn't straighten it out to push myself up anymore. I called the doctor, but he had moved on, and they didn't have anyone at the Penn State Health Milton S. Hershey Medical Center (locally called simply the Hershey Medical Center), who could see me for a couple of months. By then it would be too late to do much about the problem. Sometimes I wonder, if I could have gotten someone to look at it sooner, if it could have been helped. However, you can't second-guess things like that.

The medical people did send me to therapy to see if the therapists could improve the strength in the leg, but that didn't work.

It was 2018 when I started using the scooter. I had an old scooter at the time that wasn't in the greatest shape, but I had to fight with the insurance for a while to get a new model. Debbie helped me, and the rehab doctor helped us fill out all the paperwork correctly for the insurance company. It took about a year to finally get the new scooter.

The old one I had was a gift from Tim; it had belonged to his mother-in-law. We hadn't been planning to go to his house for Christmas that year, but Tim and Connie kept insisting that we needed to come, and it was because they had that big gift for me!

I'm always determined to keep myself going, to be doing things. The first time I couldn't walk and get to the van, I was determined that I was going to use a scooter to get to the van and slide myself into the seat. It didn't work out that way at first, but eventually I got a sense of confidence from being able to do that.

I had my pride for a while; I kept walking when I should have been using a scooter. My wife told me I should use the scooter instead. A couple of times I ended up falling in the store, and then I wished I'd used the scooter. Now I am proud to use it. That's what I have to use if I want to get around, and I do want to get out and do things.

I have my own scooter now, so I don't need to worry about whether one is available at the store or not. Walmart was the first place where I really used the scooter. My wife was with me. It's a big place to get around.

The basket on the Walmart scooter is built right in. The hardest part, once we both needed a scooter, was that the stores don't always have a group of them sitting around. Once you buy your own, though, you don't need to wait. The problem with having your own, on the other hand, is that it doesn't have the basket built in. I carry one of the baskets the store has for the customers, and that works pretty well. I think a lot of people I talk to in the store realize that, too. They can tell from my attitude about riding the scooter that it doesn't bother me.

For a while, we had an older van that had a lift in the back. My wife would load me into the back and off we'd go. My parents had bought us the lift for Christmas one year. I could still move enough that I could load myself in the beginning. Deb was lifting things in and out of the van for me. She helped me get out because we didn't have a ramp at the time. She'd go around the back of the van to help me with the lift, and she ended up falling and breaking her hip.

At first, Debbie was able to get up. She thought it was a torn muscle. But as she tried to walk around, she could tell something wasn't right. After that, we were dependent on someone else to load me into the van since she couldn't do it anymore. People didn't always have the time, so we had to work around all that.

We rode a handicapped bus for a little while when we had to, but that could be a problem as well because, if they had to pick up someone else, it could be two or more hours before the bus would come back for us. That's when Debbie was determined to do something better because she did not like to sit and wait that way.

My wife, when her mother died, received an inheritance. We decided that we would get a special van so we could do things together. The van was equipped with a ramp and had a transfer seat so I could get out and do the driving.

The van was invented by Ralph Braun, who had a spinal muscular atrophy that made it so he couldn't walk. In the early 1970s, he built a van for himself, then started making them for other people. It ended up becoming this huge company.

The van gave me my pride back.

Deb knew we wanted our freedom. We had tried the bus, but we had to wait two or three hours before it would come back and that just wasn't acceptable for us. I didn't really care for waiting for other people. I had always taken care of myself, so I didn't want to rely on anyone else. Deb also knew it would get us out to do things, too.

Our pastor once told me that so many people complain about how hard it is to get to church sometimes, maybe because it's raining or a cold day. But when they saw all that Deb and I went through to make it there, they thought that should give people incentive to maybe complain a little less.

Something Missing, Something Found

On the scooter, I would shovel snow when I needed to get to Walmart in the winter. Sometimes, while I'm on my power chair, I do think, *People, get out of the way!* If you don't watch out, people will walk right in front of you because they're not paying attention, even when you're on a power chair. Still, I do what I can to stay active and out and about.

Around that same time, my father developed dementia. Mom took care of him, but then she was hospitalized and couldn't care for him anymore. Debbie and I ended up taking care of him. We weren't really in the shape to do it either, and my brother knew that. My parents weren't taking their meds like they were supposed to, and if Mom got sick, my dad wouldn't be able to take care of her. Dad had to go to dialysis three times a week, and she would drive him early in the morning each time.

So, they moved into an assisted living place together, right across the street from where Tim lived in Lancaster, Pennsylvania. Tim would pick them up and take them to my father's dialysis appointments, and then the bus would bring them back.

It gave me comfort knowing they got to stay together.

CHAPTER THREE
A Turn for the Worse

Through the Pain
By 2019, I was helping Debbie with several medical issues. She went through heart bypass surgery around Easter of 2015. She went in for chest pain, and they found out it was from the heart. There were three blockages.

At that time, when she went in for surgery, we'd recently gotten a new pastor at our UCC church, Pastor Chris Schwab. He'd come to Carlisle by himself at first while his wife, Visitation Pastor Rachel Schwab, stayed behind and put things in order where they had lived before. So, when Pastor Rachel came to visit us in the hospital, neither of us had seen the other before. I saw a woman wandering around in the hallway and thought, *That's probably the pastor.* I went out in the hall and introduced myself, and she came into the room.

Pastor Rachel has been with us through everything, even all the issues that came after Debbie's surgery. And after that heart bypass, it seemed like the problems just continued to pile up.

Deb had anxiety, and some of the medicine affected her memory a little. I had to take care of that. The last couple of years, one of the doctors finally figured out which medicine was causing that problem and got her off it. She got a lot better then. Deb, also diabetic, was on insulin, took a lot of steroids because she had asthma, and was taking painkillers.

When my wife had anxiety and didn't want to go anywhere, I was determined to get her to go to church with me. It was hard because I know she didn't want to, but I pushed—not too hard, just a little—to get her to go. I knew she needed that.

Then she started to have trouble with her leg and couldn't do physical activities anymore, so we were at home most of the time. She'd go to some places with me, but she had to stay in the car while I went in to get whatever we were there for. Debbie was in a lot of pain, but she was determined to go with me.

It was important to go with her to the store; that was our time out. We'd make a day of it, going somewhere to eat and picking up our groceries. We were going out like everyone else. I remember us having fun looking for DVDs in the bargain bins at Walmart.

It was hard to adjust to not being able to do those things anymore.

That's where I sometimes think God knew what He was doing because, if she couldn't have gone out like that, I think that would have been too hard on us both. It helps me to know that. I know I would have wanted to stay home then, too, if she couldn't have gone. Then both of us would have been stuck never going anywhere.

The nursing profession was such a big part of who she was. I know how important it was to her. When she found that she couldn't go back to work, she was really upset.

I remember calling my mother because somebody else had to help her deal with that. I did what I could, but she needed somebody else to talk to, too. Mom also helped us fight the doctor's office to get Debbie's retirement. My mother went and found a lawyer who helped us fight and get what Debbie deserved. That's where a lot of my determination comes from—my mother was always determined like that.

It was good that Debbie got that retirement, but it didn't replace the satisfaction she got from doing her job. However, she then poured that care into me.

The one time I fell in the shower and hurt my knee, she was there for me to help me out. I got to see her as a nurse taking care of me at that time.

Our bathroom had to be handicapped accessible for us to use it, and the church took care of that. They did that for us. When I couldn't walk anymore, when I couldn't get into the shower, I had to do something different, and the church knew I couldn't afford it. They helped us.

Sometimes you just have to swallow your pride and ask for help. It's not always easy, but sometimes you have to do it.

It drove Debbie crazy that I didn't always listen to her. I think I tried to start driving the car before I should have, after my knee issues. My stubbornness wasn't always easy for her. I think that shows the patience that she had, too.

Some of the doctors where she had worked weren't very good at listening. I don't think they always liked to hear when she told them what she knew because of her hands-on contact with the patients.

Nurses are special people. They advocate for you, too, because the doctors don't always understand when you ask them questions. Nurses can help them pause and listen to you. And you have to remember that if the nurses aren't so nice or understanding, they might be having a lot going on in their own lives.

Debbie loved what she did, and later on she forgave one person, a medical professional in the practice, with whom she had an issue. We had been nervous about talking to him at church, but she forgave him, and I think he respected her for that. My wife just knew she couldn't drag that issue with her for the rest of her life. She wanted to make peace with it.

Her mother didn't always understand that. But that's a whole different story we're not going to get into! She couldn't believe Debbie did that. Her mother always held onto everything. My mother, on the other hand, gave her understanding. She embraced Debbie.

Don't get me wrong, Deb loved her mother, too, but that was just the way her mother was. And God put other people in Debbie's life who gave her other things she needed.

When you get married, whatever the family is, you're a part of it. Debbie and I made it work.

Debbie actually saw her mother die of cancer. That was hard for her as a nurse's aide. Debbie got sick right after that. I don't know that she ever grieved that loss. I never saw her cry or anything, so I don't know what went on with that. I just wonder sometimes if there was something I could have done to help her at the time. We should be ready for that. We can't know everything other people are dealing with in their hearts.

That was when things started to get worse. In November of 2019, Debbie had a vein replaced in her right leg to fix her circulation. The operation was done at Chambersburg Hospital, before Thanksgiving. I thought she was never going to get out of surgery. Finally, the doctor came and told me they were having a hard time getting it to connect, but they hoped it would work.

They kept her there for a few days and then moved her out to Green Ridge Village, which was in Newville, for therapy. It seemed to go well; her foot and the replaced vein were good then.

She had to stay over for Thanksgiving, but I was able to enjoy the day there with her. They let us eat Thanksgiving dinner together, and then, later in the evening, her brothers Barry and Don and their wives Bonnie and Linda came and brought some pumpkin pie for dessert. We got to have some family time with them.

She came home right before Christmas and the vein stayed the way it had been at Green Ridge for about a week.

Unfortunately, it didn't last. The circulation went back to the way it was.

We went to see the doctor again, who decided that they were going to have to amputate the right leg. The hospital held off on the scheduling to do the surgery because they wanted to give us the holidays.

Debbie was in so much pain at Christmas that she had a hard time enjoying it. I think she endured the pain just to be here with me. Who would have thought it would be our last Christmas together ….

That day, Debbie gave me a card that still means a lot to me. It reads:

It's a Blessing
Having a Husband
Like You

If we love each other,
God lives in us
And his love
Is made complete in us.
1 John 4:12

As long as we have
Memories to look back on
And dreams to hold onto.
As long as we have
Faith to guide us
And prayers to carry us
Through the hard times ...
As long as we have
Things to be thankful for
And laughter and smiles
Between us ...

As long as we have each other
And God's love in our hearts
We'll always have everything
We need.

I Love You.
Merry Christmas.[5]

She signed her last Christmas card, "With Love Always, Debbie."

The plan had been to do the surgery in January, but we couldn't wait. Debbie was in such pain. She just couldn't get comfortable no matter where she put her leg and could never sleep because the pain was so bad. Still, my wife hung on until after New Year's, 2020. That weekend, we packed everything up and put away all the Christmas stuff because we knew that once we went to the hospital, she wouldn't be home for a while.

That was hard.

She wanted a different opinion about the amputation, so we decided to go to the emergency room at Hershey Medical Center rather than back to Chambersburg Hospital, to see what they had to say. A doctor friend said that the fastest way to get her help was to take her to the ER, and that would get her right in.

We'd been going to visit my parents in the nursing home. They'd been there a couple of years by then. Mom was showing signs of dementia. It

---

[5] Copyright *American Greetings, Cleveland, Ohio.*

didn't really come out until she was in the home because she was very good at masking it. Dad had dementia really badly, so we didn't notice that she had it, too.

Mother never really adjusted to living at the home. When she heard about Debbie's leg problems, she was like, "Well, I can come home and take care of her!" We knew that wasn't going to happen, but it was her nature.

When things started happening with Debbie, the time I had to spend with my parents became limited. Before Debbie went to the emergency room, she told me I should go visit them. She wanted to visit as well, but she was no way in the shape to do that. They were dear to her, too. Even with all the pain my wife was in, in the hospital, she wanted to go and see Mom. However, I knew there was no way she could do it. Sometimes, I wish I would have tried harder to make that happen. I'm sure there was a way.

But I try not to think too much about what might have been.

I wanted to make sure Debbie was getting the best care possible. Where I live, Hershey Medical Center is the best place to go because they seem to be more up-to-date.

I drove her to Hershey, and we ended up having them get her a wheelchair because she couldn't walk in. There was just too much pain.

I'm very glad I took her to Hershey because the doctor there was very thorough. He explained everything. She was admitted right away. I stayed there that night because it was so late. They weren't really concerned about people staying with their loved ones at that time. It was about a week before they got all the tests back to decide on the best thing to do.

The opinion from the Hershey doctor was the same. The leg would need to be amputated.

The doctor gave us a couple of days to think about it. He said he would try to help her leg another way, but he didn't think it would work. The agreement was that if the second option wouldn't work, they would go ahead with the amputation.

I guess the word is *devastated*. We took the news hard. I was trying to console her, telling her it was okay, but it was a tough time for both of us.

I think we later came around to the idea that, since she was in so much pain, it had to be done so she wouldn't be in pain. I told her that after it was done, she'd feel better and then there wouldn't be all that pain. I put my faith in God and prayed every day. She was a praying woman, too.

Debbie stayed in the medical center for a couple of days. I drove an hour one way every day from Newville to Hershey to stay with her at the center all day. We would watch TV, some Western shows, *Walker, Texas Ranger*—she liked that. We watched *Cops*, too. The center had a cafeteria. I'd go get food for her and bring it back when it was mealtime.

Finally, the amputation was done at the Hershey Medical Center, below the right knee. The surgery took four hours. Don and Linda were there with me that day. They got to talk to her beforehand and help her through it a little, and the three of us got to see her in recovery after it was over.

Debbie was in the Hershey facility for two weeks before she had the surgery, so I was worried all that time, too. When I went to Hershey after the surgery, I always hoped I'd run into Dr. Heim, the vascular surgeon who performed the operation, and thank him for taking care of her. I never got to see him again, but I really appreciated his care. Doctors have a really hard job, and I'm sure it's good to know sometimes when their work is appreciated.

They were doing therapy at the medical center to get her ready to go to a different therapy place. Finally, they decided she would go to a facility in Mechanicsburg for that additional therapy. The idea was that at Mechanicsburg they'd work aggressively and get her better and ready to come back home. But that was just the start of it.

The night before she was supposed to come home from Mechanicsburg, something happened. Somehow, she fell and broke her other leg. That delayed the whole process because they couldn't do anything until that leg healed.

The day she broke her leg was the day she was supposed to come home for an evaluation at the house to see if she could make it on her own.

Debbie was in a lot of pain. For a while they said it wasn't broken. We had to be persistent for a day or so to go back to the doctor and get the x-ray done. I went in and said something about it because I knew it had to be done. There was a doctor whom Debbie was working with who was good at that sort of thing. The x-ray proved it was broken. With her good leg broken, she couldn't do anything, so she had to go back into therapy. That delayed everything.

I guess I can admit now that for a while I was mad and wanted to sue, but my wife calmed me down. Debbie said she didn't need that. She was the one who was injured, yet she still wanted to see the better side. I figured I'd better back off with that idea.

In the end, I think not suing was the right decision. A lawsuit probably wouldn't have done us any good; it would have just stressed us out. But sometimes I can get rather excited about those kinds of things.

I think that, through all of this, I have more patience now than I did before. Debbie taught me that.

When the garage had trouble with our car and I got mad and started screaming at the manager, she calmed me down. I'm not proud of losing my temper like that, but I used to do that. I can take some things for so long, and then I've had enough.

Now, I've learned to handle things like that with more patience and explain myself calmly because yelling doesn't help. The other person just gets upset more.

Sometimes it makes us feel better, though.

After all that, the facility called and told me they couldn't do the therapy anymore, so Debbie was transferred to the Claremont Nursing and Rehabilitation Center in Carlisle. Claremont was a good facility. She had a friend who was there at the same time, and they were able to eat lunch together while she was there.

Debbie stayed at the nursing facility for a couple of weeks, and the leg got infected again. She went back to Hershey, and they said they would treat the infection. Then I got a call about one o'clock in the morning informing me that they were going to have to take it above the knee. Another amputation. That was hard to hear.

I drove in and spent the night in her room. They weren't sure when the doctor would come in, and I wanted to be there to talk to him.

During that second surgery, we almost lost her.

I remember that there were five doctors in the room. They let me stay in the room as long as I stood far enough back that I was out of their way. I guess they thought, in case something happened, I should be there.

Through all of this I learned to be a patient advocate and ask the doctors questions. Sometimes we weren't really sure what they were doing and had to ask a lot of questions. I did that for her because I really loved her and wanted to make sure things were done correctly. Sometimes the doctors would say, "Oh, we're going to send her home," when I thought it wasn't really time to go home yet.

I learned a lot about health insurance, too.

Being there for someone and being that advocate is very important. There were times when I needed to make phone calls and other times when I had to get there before visiting hours started to catch the doctor because sometimes they'd be there really early. Our local hospital didn't push strict visiting hours that much, so you could go in early and catch the doctor.

After the second operation, they moved her to Cumberland Crossings, an assisted living community also in Carlisle, where they had a therapy facility. Her leg was starting to heal to the point where they could do a little therapy.

Debbie always worked so hard on rehabilitation because she wanted to come home and be with me.

Long Drives and Loving Days

While Debbie was going through all these surgeries and rehab, I was there with her every day. She always said my long visit was the best part of her day.

I listened to music on my hour-long drives, and I found that gave me some comfort. But when I left, I still had that hour-long drive back home. That was the hardest time, knowing I was going home but she wasn't coming home with me. It took a toll on me. I really don't know how I kept myself awake all those drives, either. Luckily, it didn't snow a lot that winter.

But I always knew that, the next day, I was going to go back.

On those long drives, I thought about everything that could have gone wrong and everything that had to be taken care of. A lot of the time, I'd turn the car radio on just to relax, to take away some of that pressure. I loved the country radio station, FM 102.3. I've always liked country music, especially Shania Twain's songs.

The van was a big help. It allowed me to still have my independence, which was very important to me. Early on, when Debbie was having troubles and I still had the old vehicle, I had to rely on somebody to come and meet me and help me unload to go see her at the hospital. I didn't get to come see her as much as I wanted to during that time.

I remember one time when she was first at the hospital and I had the old vehicle, I could only stay for an hour. She thought I could stay longer. I remember her crying when I left.

Of course, I was crying, too. But I tried not to show that when I was there.

In the rehab facility, every time I'd see Debbie, she tried to make the best of it. She tried to enjoy all the activities, the bingo, things like that. She always found the brighter side.

All during that time, I wasn't working. Honestly, I probably would have lost any job I had because I couldn't keep my mind on anything but Debbie. I'd have tried to work, but there would have been no way. I was giving Debbie my undivided attention. That's what gives me peace, now. I don't have any regrets that I was distracted by other things.

Even with everything she went through, she still had a smile on her face. That was the best thing, always seeing her smile. Debbie gave that to me. She showed me how to not give up.

I was praying every day, and I felt like my prayers were going to be answered with Debbie recovering and coming home. I was so focused on her that I wasn't getting to church services, either. I didn't want my wife to be alone on Sunday. The pastor would come and see her. She gave us words of encouragement and prayed with us. That helped.

I made sure Debbie had her laundry done. When she got to the rehab facility, they didn't do the laundry there. In the nursing home, she still wanted me to do it because they didn't always get the stains out.

She also wanted her Dr. Pepper, and I'd bring one in for her. She liked word find booklets, so I'd bring those in to her, too.

The medical center didn't really limit hours. Because of the amputation, they felt like she needed the visits, so they didn't push that. Now, I think I probably should have left earlier sometimes because it could be really late by the time I got home.

In the morning, I'd leave and stop at McDonald's for breakfast, then arrive at the center around 9:00 a.m. I wanted to catch the doctor and hear what he had to say, and he was there early in the morning. I made sure to be there because I was her patient advocate. She couldn't always remember what they told her, so I wanted to hear it from them. I knew I had to be there early.

I'd stay through lunch and supper. There was a cafeteria that had sandwiches and other food. It was à la carte, where you could pick up different kinds of things, almost like a mini restaurant in the building. I'd pick up some food and take the items back to her and we'd have lunch.

We usually watched TV and talked. She liked to watch *Walker, Texas Ranger* and *The Andy Griffith Show*. That was a good show for us because Andy and his Mayberry friends put us in a good place. She had a whole set of DVDs of *Walker, Texas Ranger*, too. Cordell Walker, Chuck Norris's character, was one of my heroes on TV. He could be tough but then be compassionate, too.

Before I would leave, I'd say goodbye, give her a kiss, and tell her I loved her. She'd say the same thing back. She knew I'd be coming back the next day.

When I left, I'd hide my emotions, knowing it would upset her. It was hard to leave at night. She probably was holding in her feelings, too.

Sometimes I'd fall asleep there. It got to be a long day after a while. My health was mostly good, but I wasn't getting a lot of rest. I didn't sleep that great at night, so I could be very tired sometimes. I didn't take care of myself like I should have. I was supposed to be doing exercises with my legs, and I didn't do that. That's what I'm catching up on now. But Debbie understood I needed to take care of her at that time. Most people would have done that.

The nurses came in while I was there. Some of them I got along with pretty well. I asked them questions. Some of the nurses were good at answering and explaining. I needed the comfort of knowing she was being taken care of.

When my wife was a nurse's aide, I didn't always understand why she stayed so late at her work. I never had a job that I loved the way she loved nursing. Sometimes on a Friday night, I'd want to do something and be like, "Are you going to get home?" Sometimes I was understanding, but not always. She'd call and say, "I'll be a while yet," and that wasn't always easy.

But when we were on the other side of nursing, I saw why she worked those long hours. It was to take care of those patients. That care that she gave, she got it back, in more ways than one.

I think that was why Debbie was more understanding of the doctors and nurses we dealt with. She was in that profession, and it was part of who she was.

All that was before they moved her to Cumberland Crossings. I got to see her the first day she moved in there.

And then … COVID-19 came.

Lockdown

I'd been focused all this time on my wife. COVID was starting to be talked about on the news, but it seemed like something far away, like it was other people's problem. I knew at the time that they were talking about shutting things down, but it wasn't really apparent that they were going to do it yet. It seemed like it would be some days before they did anything. I kind of denied it for a while, thinking that it was more in other areas, that it wasn't here.

The last day I was able to visit her, the COVID crisis was coming. We were at the hospital, and they were transferring her over to the new rehab center at Hershey. I waited until that was done. I could sense something was different.

That was the last time I got to see her there.

I had a cold and had to hide it because I didn't want anybody to hear me cough. I was drowning it in cough drops, determined that I was going to be with her. I could have gotten in trouble, but, luckily, I didn't. It made me wonder later if I had a minor case of COVID back then, but they tested me and told me it was the regular flu.

The second day she was in for therapy, I was just getting ready to go when they called and said they weren't allowing anybody in the building because of the virus. I was really worried about telling Debbie I couldn't come. Then she called me and shared with me that I wasn't going to be able to come anymore. That took a weight off of me, that I didn't have to tell her. Even so, it was a really hard thing for me to accept. I was used to visiting her, to making that drive every day. I know it was hard for her, too.

What I thought at the time was that this crisis would last only a couple of months and then everything would be back to normal. That wasn't how it turned out.

Every morning, I woke up, turned on the news and listened to them keep talking about how many people died each day. The restaurants shut down; only takeout was allowed. Everyone was supposed to wear masks everywhere, although I was stubborn about that at first. The world was turned upside-down, and it seemed like it happened overnight.

I was still praying every day. I thought everything was going to be okay. Because of COVID, I didn't get into contact with a lot of people, but I know they were praying for us, too.

After about four weeks, Debbie was transferred over to Cumberland Crossing. Debbie and I found a way to make do—the phone would keep us together. We would talk for hours. The staff were okay with that because they knew we were talking. Usually I got the phone call in the morning. First thing when I got up, she was calling to talk to me. That phone call was really important, and that's the part I miss the most.

Our conversations could last a couple of hours or more every day. We used a prepaid phone, so we had to keep buying more minutes. It always needed more time. The worst part is when you run out in the middle of a call and have to get more minutes. Our phone calls could last for hours on end. I'd end up running the minutes out on the prepaid phone every couple of nights. At first, I used the pin cards from the stores, but then I did learn how to get minutes on the computer. Then I didn't have to go to the store for the cards. That was one thing I got determined to do then: get a regular cell phone so I wouldn't have to buy any more minutes in the middle of a call.

Luckily, my cell phone was more unlimited. Finally, the nurses saw the problem residents were having and put free phones in the rooms for everybody. Usually they charged for that service, but the staff realized people needed to communicate. Once Debbie got the phone set up, we could use our house phone, too. At that time, I still had the landline. I've gotten rid of that now, though.

The facility did offer Zoom back then, but we didn't know anything about that, so we didn't try it. I took a course a long time ago in computers, but that was way back around 2009. This was a whole different kind of thing. I probably could have figured it out, but Debbie would have had a harder time.

The most important thing was that we were able to hear each other's voices.

We'd talk about what was going on that day, what she was doing there, what I was doing at home, and even what the cat was doing, too. Sometimes I'd hold up the phone to the cat so she could talk to Sweetie, and sometimes Sweetie would talk back. Debbie always wanted to try. I think she was trying to lighten up my spirits. She'd find things she needed for me to look for in the store, things for her room, and I think sometimes that was just to keep me busy, to give me something to do.

My wife was still being a caregiver.

Sometimes there was a football game on. She was a big Pittsburgh Steelers fan. We would get on the phone and watch the whole game, cheering the Steelers on together. Sometimes one of us would talk when the other wanted to hear something on the TV, but we were still there with each other over the phone.

The biggest thing she was proud of was finishing in third place in the facility's weekly football picking pool. Her picks were tied for first in week three! Debbie said that comes from having three brothers and having to learn some football. She ended up teaching me a lot about the game over the years.

She also liked to watch the NASCAR races. Kyle Busch was her favorite driver.

Debbie would share what was going on at the facility. The staff called bingo from the hall, when people had to stay in the rooms. Debbie had a couple of roommates who didn't work out so well, and we'd talk about that. But then, in the end, she got a roommate whom she liked, and then they could talk. At first, they put her in the room with somebody who had a lot of problems and didn't really talk, and that's hard to do to someone. It wasn't that person's fault, of course; that lady couldn't help it. But that was hard for Deb.

Once the roommate situation got worked out, it gave me some comfort to know she had someone to talk to when I wasn't around. I think she stood up for herself to get a good roommate. Debbie learned she had to do some advocacy for herself because I couldn't be there to speak up like I did before. I like to think that all those little pushes I gave her over the years helped her with that.

I did get to see her for a second time. I came in for an evaluation to see if I could take her home and take care of her. But when the meeting was over, they didn't think I could handle that level of care yet. At that time, I still had the hope that she was coming home. I kept thinking that every day.

Debbie had an appointment at an allergy office every other week, and they knew I always went there with her and so let me keep sitting in for those. They probably weren't supposed to do that, but they did it anyhow. The staff there were a little more lenient on that sort of thing. But we weren't allowed to touch. So many times, I just wanted to hold her hand at the doctors' appointments. But they didn't want you to do that because of COVID, because it would spread.

She had one doctor who would delay a little bit before calling for the nursing home van. So, we would have a little time together. And one of the drivers would wait a little while before she would leave. The nursing home may not have liked that either, but these kind people just saw that we needed those moments. She had been in for surgery for other things before, so they knew our relationship, too.

We needed to see each other. The big thing was, she'd make sure I'd wear the mask when I went up because I didn't want to get COVID.

The rest of the time, I kept myself busy. I had prescriptions and other things I needed to get. In the beginning, you couldn't find anything at Walmart; all the shelves were empty. I was a little stubborn about wearing a mask then, but finally I realized that people had to, that it wasn't really a choice. You had to go out and protect yourself the best way you knew how, but then the store didn't have everything you needed.

I remember that, even with the lockdown, I brought Debbie's clothes home and washed them. Being in a nursing home for rehab, they don't provide a laundry service. However, there was a special day I could go in to drop clean clothes off and pick up the dirty laundry. Those times were limited; they didn't want people coming too often. Luckily, I had the special handicapped van by then. I remember that, during those months, there was hardly any traffic on the turnpike and a driver could make record time. There was nobody there to bother you—you could just go!

I know I was taking a risk with COVID at the time (I really realize it now!), but she needed laundry done. That was when we were still thinking it would only be a couple of months before we'd be back to normal.

Eventually, when COVID got bad, the facility wouldn't let me come in and get the wash. The staff would leave it at the front door, and family members would have to come get it. Later, they weren't sure if even doing it that way was spreading the virus, so they hired a laundry company to come in and do it instead. That was hard because I wanted to take care of that for her.

The main issue was that Debbie really liked her Dr. Pepper, so I always went to the store and got that for her, too. She had to have her soda. Cumberland Crossings had a table where you dropped stuff off for family members. If people wanted things, family were allowed in the building to leave it for them on the table. But with COVID, even Debbie's soda got hard to find for a while. And I couldn't stock up on it because customers were only allowed to get two packs at the store.

I could see why people did that. One time at Walmart, they found somebody who was buying a whole bunch of milk. It turned out that the person had a convenience store and was buying up all that milk so to sell it in his own store. They finally caught the man and figured it out. He was probably inflating the price in his store, too.

Some people just take advantage.

Sometimes I could get everything I needed. Toilet paper was the hardest to get. For my septic tank, I needed to have a certain brand. I could only get a different kind of toilet paper, one that wouldn't break down the way it needed to for my tank. A couple of times I ended up having to pay for somebody to come out and unclog the septic system because I didn't have the right paper, but I didn't really have a choice.

Things were getting worse with Mom and Dad's conditions, too. Before the lockdown, I know they wanted to see me, but I had to take care of my wife. My plate was full. Tim stepped in and dealt with the issues they were facing. He still got to see them when the virus was around because he had to pick them up for Dad's dialysis appointments.

As Mom dealt more and more with dementia, she began to want to come home every day. That was her place; that was where she wanted to be. Her and my dad built their home together. They were there for about fifty years. But that just wasn't practical.

I don't think she understood that. A couple of times she almost made it out, too. She'd call a taxi, and then the nurses would see what was going on and catch her before she left. My dad, in his condition, wasn't really bothered by where he was at. He'd actually ask, "Where is home?"

My brother would call and tell me how things were going with our parents. The problem was, when Mom would call, she wanted to come home, and I couldn't really take that stress at that time.

After a while, when she would call on the phone, I wouldn't answer because I knew what she was going to ask. I had so much stress with Debbie, I just couldn't handle that. I'm not proud of my response, but people could tell her over and over what the situation was, and she just wouldn't listen. I think it was better that I didn't answer because I would get upset and say things that I wouldn't mean.

I guess, in the nursing home, her wanting to go home was her way of fighting even then. It was just so hard on the rest of us. Tim was trying to be there for us as well as for his church members.

I sort of stopped thinking about myself and my health. I ate a lot of fast food then, but there were some days when I'd only eat one meal a day. I know I held in a lot of emotional turmoil at that time. I guess I felt back then that I didn't have the time to cry.

My attorney had been trying to get someone to come and help out, so that we could maybe bring her home, but with COVID, we never did find anyone.

I remember being excited about our first anniversary. Then, before we knew it, we were celebrating our twenty-third. She was in the nursing home for our twenty-fourth anniversary on April 19. I still took red roses and an anniversary card to her there. Red roses were her favorite. She felt bad because she couldn't get a card to send me. I told her she didn't need to feel bad about that.

I'd look at a letter I had written to her a while back that she had hanging on the wall on her side of the bedroom. The letter was just a little thing, but it meant a lot to her. It read:

LOVE IS
When you have a partner who listens to you.
There through the hard times.
Loves to laugh at your jokes
Forgives you when you say things you shouldn't.
Supports you.
Just having fun going out to dinner or movies.
Sharing quiet moments.
Getting together with family.
Sharing going to Church and choir together.
Enjoying movies at home on our big screen.
Making wonderful meals and desserts.

Thanks, Debbie
You're all that and more.

Love you, Jim.

Love you very much. I always want to be there for you through thick and thin.

Debbie was my hero. All those bad breaks hit her life, and she still kept going.

And then, a couple of weeks before Thanksgiving, she got COVID.

CHAPTER FOUR
Then, the Rains Came

One of Millions

I did get to see Debbie at the allergist appointment a couple of days before she died. I bought her a new Pittsburgh Steelers zip-up sweatshirt. I'm pretty sure she had it on that day. She really liked that I got that for her.

All those months in this routine of her at the facility, we'd kept busy and kept our spirits up. COVID was disrupting everything, but the virus was only something that happened to other people, we believed. And then came the diagnosis.

I got a call from Cumberland Crossings—I think it was Saturday. They said they had to take her over to the local hospital, UPMC at Carlisle, formerly the Carlisle Regional Medical Center. Her breathing was bad, but at that point they weren't sure what it was yet.

I went to the ER, but the staff told me I couldn't come in. So, I called Don and Linda, and they told me to come over to their house in Carlisle and wait with them until we found out what was going on.

It was about two or three hours before the medical staff came back with the results of the quick test. They called me on my cell phone and told me that Debbie had COVID. It was a shock. The three of us tried to deny it at first. Maybe we denied a little that she had it, but certainly that it would get worse. We told ourselves that things would work out.

We prayed together. We called Pastor Chris. He said he'd be thinking and praying for us. I know now that he was probably praying for a lot of other people in the same situation. I stayed with Don and Linda, and we had supper and talked for a while.

Eventually Debbie got moved to her room and she called me, wanting me to go get her belongings from the nursing home. The hospital gave her a bunch of steroids to get her breathing under control, and she was all wound up. Deb wanted her Dr. Pepper!

It was late at night, but I went and got the soda, then dropped it off at the hospital to be taken up to her. It was hard to just drop it off and leave; I really wanted to go up and see her. That was a hard day.

Debbie denied that she had COVID for a couple of days. I guess she didn't want to think it was true. Maybe she didn't want me to worry about it. She thought she was going to go back to the nursing home in a couple of days and told me that the doctor had said that to her.

She was diabetic, had asthma and had had heart bypass surgery years before, so that meant she already had a lot of risk factors that would make it harder for her to recover.

People kept calling me and asking for updates. Everything I heard from the hospital was that she was doing well. We just kept thinking that she was going to pull out of it.

Debbie fought it for a whole week. As I've said before, that's where some of my fight comes from, for I saw how she fought—just like my mom. We're a family of fighters.

They gave her meds that were supposed to help, and she did well for a while, but then it went the other way.

I think I was trying not to see it. I think I was denying it. So many times, she went through physical problems and came back from them, and I was telling myself that it was going to happen again. One day, she said they tried to get her up, but she didn't have the strength like she did before to do that. But still, I was optimistic.

We kept calling each other up until the end. We'd talk an hour or so every day.

There wasn't anyone in the room with her. She didn't really understand why the nurses weren't coming in very often. She didn't realize that the nurses were limited in the amount of time they were allowed to be in there with COVID.

Debbie—all the patients who had it—were isolated.

The Friday after she was admitted, she was still okay. The next day, Saturday, when I talked to her, she was like a completely different person. She wasn't quite as responsive and upbeat as she was before. Her voice was lower. She had been looking forward to going back to the nursing home, but the doctor had told her they wouldn't take her back for a while because of COVID. She seemed to go straight downhill after that.

On the phone, Debbie told me to keep wearing a mask so I wouldn't get it because, she said, "You don't want to get this." So, she was still thinking of me, even then. And I listened.

On our last call, we talked about the inner strength she had, her faith. When I talked to her that last time, I said, "You better come home soon." She said, "What are you talking about?" I think she knew that was going to be the last day. She was kind of in and out. The thing that hurts the most is that I yelled at her and told her to stay awake so I could talk to her. "Don't do this to me; I need you!" I said.

She was crying, but she was also in and out.

From what happened later, I think she talked to her brother toward the end and told him to make sure I was going to be okay.

The day before, I called and called. It was hard to get ahold of a nurse, and callers couldn't talk at that time. I don't quite understand what happened that day. I guess the nurses were busy. Sometimes I'd let the phone ring and ring, and the nurses wouldn't answer. When someone did, I'd hear, "That's not my patient. I'm not allowed to go in that room." I don't think it was the nurses' fault; there were so many patients and so little staff.

At that time, I thought differently. Now, I understand. I just really wanted to know what was going on.

The next day, I was able to get through. They told me that the nurse was in the room. That was all they told me. I guess they were working on her, trying to help, but I didn't realize it then.

During those days after she got the diagnosis is when I really started questioning my faith. The answers to my prayers were not the answers

I wanted. It had been almost a year since she was home with me. I was praying and doing everything I was supposed to do, so why couldn't this be fixed for me? Why did it happen? Why couldn't she have been home before it all happened?

I'd prepared for her to come home, everyone told me she was coming home, and they were praying for that, too. But now I doubted. I felt like God wasn't helping, so I would fix it myself. I'd work harder to fix up the house.

On Sunday, they started breathing treatments. They put her on a machine, one like a CPAP (Continuous Positive Airway Pressure) machine, to try and get her breathing. They were trying to do all they could to get her breathing without intubating her, but they told me on Monday that a couple of times her heart stopped, and they had to bring her back.

The medical professionals did the best they could with what they had at the time. They were limited in what they could do, in what they knew to do.

I remembered a time when she'd been in the hospital before. Debbie was unresponsive for about a day, at that time. I don't know what the problem was, but I didn't know if she was going to come back. That was a scary time. The whole family was in her room, trying to talk to her and get her to come back. She finally did.

I hung onto the idea that it would happen this time, too.

The Calls

On the 17th of November, at about one o'clock in the morning, I got a call from the hospital. They were going to start ventilating her. Her body just couldn't take it anymore. They needed my permission, and I said yes.

They told me to stay close to the phone. It wasn't going to be long after that. The worst part was that, with COVID, loved ones couldn't even go and be part of those last hours.

My life was going to change forever.

I grabbed the wedding picture and held it all the rest of that night.

I prayed that it would be over then.

I picked up the phone when it rang one time, and it was my brother-in-law. I talked to my sister-in-law about how we were so scared. I know they were trying to hold it together for me.

I think what I was most scared of was being without her.

I got a call at about 11:00 in the morning to come in.

She had passed.

I ran into the wall with my scooter because I was so sad. The hole I made is still there. I think I just kept repeating "no … no …" the whole time.

Yelling, crying out.

I called my brother. I remember telling him I lost my best friend.

I didn't know at the time what he was dealing with that day, too.

For a long time after, I didn't even go back into the room where I took that call. I didn't even think about why; I just didn't want to be there. That was where my heart had broken.

Finally, somehow, I got in the van and drove to the hospital. There was no way around it. I had to go. I had to deal with it. I just grabbed my coat and went. It was breezy and drizzling a little bit.

It took about a half hour to get there. I cried the whole way in. I don't know how I even saw the road. I think that I just leaned on the steering wheel and stared at the lines on the road, not even seeing what was ahead. If anybody would have been in front of me, I would have just stopped.

I guess God was with me on that drive. How I even got there is a fog.

The hospital let us go to see her, but we couldn't go in the room. We were able to be in the hallway outside the room. They did let us do that. Pastor Rachel came in first. My brother-in-law had called her, but she had already left. She said, "I don't care what they say about COVID; I'm going with you either way." Debbie's family came, too, then: Don and Linda and Bonnie, Barry's wife. Her brother Barry was having serious issues of his own and couldn't be there. In fact, they didn't even tell him about his sister that day because they thought it wouldn't be good for him.

The doctor told us first what happened. He said that when they intubated her, when they inserted the tube, her heart just couldn't take it.

We weren't allowed to enter, only to sit outside the room in the hall and look through the glass to see her. The medical staff had already taken care of all the tubes and other equipment, so I didn't have to see that. That was a blessing in a way. The three hours I sat there, I kept looking for her to look at me and smile like she always did. I had no sense of time. I didn't even realize I was there that long. I thought my life was over.

One nurse did make sure to tell me that she had been there the whole time. So one of Debbie's fellow nurses had been there with her when she died. That did make me feel a little better. I wish I remembered this nurse's name, but everything was a fog at that time.

We sat there until about 3:00 p.m. They let me stay as long as I wanted because I was just in shock at that time. They understood that I had to stay. The pastor stayed as long as she could with me. Then her phone started lighting up because there were other people she had to deal with, too—families with family members who had also passed away from COVID.

Finally, Don gave me a nudge, saying it was time. He said I could go back to their house for a while after I went to make the funeral arrangements. I stayed with Don and Linda for a few hours. They were concerned about me going home by myself, but at that time that was all I wanted.

I remember somebody asking me if I wanted somebody to drive me home. I mentioned my brother, and he had to come up with an excuse and tell me it was because of COVID that he couldn't come up to get me. He didn't want to tell me what was happening with our mother.

They knew not to do that.

Actually, I didn't want anybody to go home with me. I just wanted to go home alone and deal with myself that night.

I was lost when I got home.

The quiet.

Debbie called from the nursing home every day, and I wouldn't have that anymore.

This was not happening.

This was not real.

The first night, it was like it didn't happen.

Sweetie sat that first night meowing in the kitchen, waiting for Debbie to come back.

Then, the Rains Came

I could have stayed in bed the next day, but I knew she wouldn't want me to do that. My parents wouldn't want that, either.

Then, my brother called me about my mother.

She had died.

It was natural causes, but I don't think it would have happened that way if not for COVID. When people couldn't come to visit her anymore, she just didn't understand. I think that was when she started to give up.

Tim actually knew Mom was dying the day my wife died, but he didn't want to tell me. It would have been too hard, and he didn't want to put that burden on me.

Mother and Debbie had always been so close, the only comfort was that neither knew the other had passed.

Now they were together. In a better place.

At the funeral home, they allowed the family to pick out favorite songs and have the music played at the viewing. Debbie liked the song, "The Lord's Prayer." The funeral home also let us show special pictures, too, in a video-type presentation. My brother-in-law helped, since she was his sister, with some of the special things he remembered.

I made sure Debbie had her Pittsburgh Steelers shirt on when she was buried—the whole Steelers outfit. We never talked about it, but I just knew to do that. I knew that was what she'd want. Her brother was a little bit stricter about her being all dressed up, but her sister-in law said, "That's the way she was comfortable the last few years; that's the way you should do it." She understood why we had to do that.

We were going to have a service in the church, but November was when things had to shut back down again. So then the funeral home offered their place. That was the plan if the church closed—the funeral home was where we'd go. There were some members in our church who had died earlier who couldn't have any kind of service because it wasn't allowed yet, but we were at least able to have that.

At Deb's funeral, Pastor Rachel sang a solo of a lovely hymn (the congregation sang the same song at Mom's funeral):

You who dwell in the shelter of the Lord,
who abide in his shadow for life,
say to the Lord: "My refuge, my rock in whom I trust!"

> *And he will raise you up on eagle's wings,*
> *bear you on the breath of dawn,*
> *make you to shine like the sun,*
> *and hold you in the palm of his hand.*
>
> *The snare of the fowler will never capture you,*
> *and famine will bring you no fear:*
> *under his wings your refuge,*
> *his faithfulness your shield.*

And the last verse:

> *For to the angels he's given a command*
> *to guard you in all of your ways;*
> *upon their hands they will bear you up,*
> *lest you dash your foot against a stone.*[6]

Not as many of her friends were able to come because of COVID, and some of them were nurses, too.

On her side of the grave marker is the image of a cat, since Sweetie liked to lie down with her. On the other side there's a deer; I always liked deer. And then there's a mountain scene, like the deer is coming out of the woods.

In the middle of the marker are the names we called each other. She always called me Jimmy, and I always called her Debbie.

I picked this poem to be a part of the service. I think that was a sign. I just picked it out, and I didn't even know it was about me. But it came to be over time.

Miss Me, But Let Me Go
When I come to the end of the road
And the sun has set for me,
I want no rites in a gloom-filled room.
Why cry for a soul set free?

---

[6] "On Eagle's Wings," © 1979 Jan Michael Joncas, published by OCP, http://catholichymn.blogspot.com/2015/07/on-eagles-wings.html?_sm_au_=iVVZsMTFK6NrQsW5V377jK0qWqcB0.

Miss me a little, but not too long,
And not with your head bowed low.

Remember the love that we once shared,
I'd like to leave an echo whispering
Miss me but let me go.

For this is a journey we all must take,
And each must go alone.
It's all part of the Master plan,
A step on the road to home.
When you are lonely and sick of heart,
Go to the friends we know
And bury your sorrows in doing good deeds.
Miss me, but let me go.[7]

We had my mother's funeral at the church that she and my father had attended. It was about fifteen minutes from our house—a small country church, but a beautiful place, with stained-glass windows. It felt like going back home in a way. I know it was home to them, too. With the church being out in the country, it was further away from the COVID situation as well; there weren't so many people watching over us.

Because of COVID, we didn't bring my father to these funerals. He had dementia, so we were afraid attending would set him off more than anything.

The Holidays
At first people told me, "You're going to go on and do stuff," but I didn't believe them at the time. "Oh, you'll date somebody and meet somebody." I never believed that was going to happen. I told Pastor Rachel that I was losing everyone I loved.

But you're reading this book, so you know I got through those dark days. You can get through them, too. Don't give up. Keep positive. Find that hero.

At the beginning, the quiet was hard. I wanted the TV on all night

---
[7] Author Unknown.

because I couldn't stand it. It had been quiet without her for so long before, but it was a different kind of quiet after she was gone. There were just things going through my head, and I wanted the TV on to try and drown out those thoughts.

I just wanted God to take me, too. Then Debbie and me, we could be together. But I don't think life is made to work out that way. At that time, I didn't care. My life was over, so what did I have to live for?

God had taken my best friend, my wife, my partner.

I didn't even have time to grieve my mom. I missed her, but I couldn't even begin to get past that. Debbie and me, we had plans, things we thought we'd have time to do.

I got angry.

I would keep screaming at Him, "Why did this have to happen?" I would be at home, screaming at the top of my lungs. "Why did You have me do all this stuff? Fix everything up?" I'd yell at Him. "It didn't do any good!"

But He didn't ask me to do those things. I was just trying to be the fixer.

Now, I look at it all as part of the plan, and a part of the plan is for me to learn that I am not in control. And that's hard. From childhood, we're taught to plan—to plan out our lives decades before—but all our plans are always subject to His plan.

I knew things would be different when she came home, but I had plans for that. Those plans didn't work out.

I was hurt.

I felt like God was punishing me.

After a couple of days, a cardinal came to the window. That was the first time I was able to turn the TV off and go to sleep. Seeing that cardinal brought me comfort and peace in a different way.

When it is quiet, it's like you can hear your voice in your head. It's hard to explain, but it's special. God knew exactly what I needed. He always does, but we don't always see it. I still didn't see it at the time.

Tim would come up to visit me during the week and bring food. We would talk and share memories of Debbie and our mother. We decided that we wanted to hang onto the family place for as long as we could. He told me that, at the nursing home, he'd found all kinds of notes and maps of Mom's plans to escape and get back home. I appreciated that my sister-in-law Connie gave him the space to be with me during those tough times for both of us.

I went through two holidays right after it happened: Thanksgiving and Christmas.

I always wanted to get out of the house; I was just afraid to do it. When I did get out, I wasn't really any happier than when I was in the house. I knew I'd have to go back in and face what was still there.

For the first time, while taking a ride where we used to go, I had to stop halfway there, sit in the car and cry. A couple of times when I started out, I had to pull the car over and just let the feelings out. It would have been dangerous to keep driving when those feelings overwhelmed me. In life we have to do that; we have to stop and take the time to feel our emotions.

The hardest thing for me was to ignore my need to see people. It was all I wanted to do. But we had to stay locked down to keep what happened to my loved ones from happening to others. It was awfully lonely, but we had to do it.

I did a lot of praying. However, I don't know that I was really talking to God anymore at that time, honestly. I was just going through the motions. I felt like, "Why pray?" It didn't help before. He wasn't going to bring her back.

It was around Christmastime when I was at Walmart by myself for the first time. I decided that I wanted to make sure I had Christmas cards so I could send some to Tim, Connie and Andrew.

I remember how the grief hit me when I was there. All around me were couples shopping together, and I wanted that so badly. By the time I got to the register, I was crying, and the checker asked me what was wrong. We talked about it. She had compassion for me and told me things would get better.

I could have just run out of the store and not gotten the card, but I wasn't going to do that. To this day, this checker will ask me how I am if I see her.

Later on, at a local grocery store, I ran into a checker who didn't know what had happened. She asked, "Where's Debbie?" She always remembered us coming in as a couple, and she and my wife would talk.

I remember not being able to say much. I just had to go. Then I ran into her at Walmart, and she helped me take my groceries out to the car.

It was hard to tell people.

I happened to run into one of the nurses at Target when I was really going through this grief, and that was hard. When you see those people who were there, it really comes back and hits you like a wave.

I told her how much I miss being able to shop with Debbie, and she said, "I know that." A lot of the workers there loved her, too. She had that sense of humor, and they loved that. Not all the patients in there appreciate what the staff do sometimes. It's important to remember to be patient with the nurses, too.

I wrote a thank-you note to the nursing home. I was able to write down my thoughts about how they had helped her, what they did for her. It helped me to send that.

By this time, COVID-19 was starting to get really bad. So, there were a lot of people who knew what I was going through because they had lost some of their family members, too. Once I lost Debbie, the pandemic became real to me. I'd thought it was just something other people were facing and would never affect me. Boy, was I so wrong.

The first few times I went out to get groceries and other items, it was tough to come back home. I could see Sweetie in the window, waiting for someone to come home. The cat would give me a reason to come back home at first.

I think what gave me the courage to go back out was that I didn't want to stay in the house. To be honest, I didn't want to go out, either. Actually, I didn't know what I wanted. But I had to do something.

One day, I caught myself just buying things, trying to deal with my feelings. I remember asking myself, *Do I really need this stuff?* I did put some of it back. I knew I was buying those things as a way to cope.

When I got up in the morning, what made me even go through the motions of shaving and taking care of myself was the thought of my family members and how they wouldn't want me to go out looking like that.

There were some days I didn't really want to get up.

At night when you fall asleep, you don't have to think about what is happening. But when you wake up in the morning, you have to think about it again. I didn't have a goal anymore. I just wanted all the pain to be over. I didn't see a life on the other side of my grief. I stopped caring for myself so much. What did it matter?

The first couple of weeks after the funeral, your family is around, looking after you. Then they start going away, and the loneliness kicks in. My friends and family said they want to be there for me—and they do want to be there for me—but life goes on for them, and it's hard to reach out when you need help.

Tim came and helped me put the tree up. I really didn't want to do it at first because of those ornaments. So many of them reminded me of people I'd just lost. But we did it.

The hard part about it was that a lot of the memories we talked about were the things my wife and I would do together. How every year we'd try to get something different in the store to put on the tree. Or when we were on vacation, how we'd find something for the tree and put it on special. For a number of years, at Christmas, our families would give us different ornaments for the tree. There are so many memories tied up in those ornaments. My sister-in-law, Connie, started that family tradition of giving ornaments. It was hard to figure out what to get for people, but the ornament tradition was good. Now, we can remember when we look at the tree.

Tim and his family were planning to come up around Christmas, but then my nephew got COVID. They had to quarantine, so they couldn't come visit. I wanted them to be here, I needed them to be here, but they couldn't take the chance.

At the time, you didn't know if you could end up with it, either. And there were mixed messages from the authorities, so you didn't know what you could and couldn't do.

One day I would feel good, and then the next day the waves of grief would come back again. It was a roller coaster. Up one minute, down the next, even within the same day. The same hour. One minute you feel great, and then the next minute, it hits you again. It doesn't happen as much now to me, but it still happens.

Right before Christmas, I knew I couldn't do it anymore without some support.

I remember not being able to sit still. I couldn't walk to pace, but I used to use the scooter. Eventually, I wore myself out. I just didn't want to think about Debbie's passing and being alone. I was trying to find a way to not think about it, but that makes the feelings worse. I thought I could do that, but it doesn't work.

I was depressed. It was a hard place to be.

Nothing I was doing worked.

I questioned everything. I always went to church; I did what God wanted—or at least I thought I did. I thought He left me.

But, He was holding me all the time, collecting my tears until I was ready for help.

Reach Out for the Strength You Need

One night, I knew I couldn't do it on my own anymore. I knew I needed help.

When I started reaching out, I had a little anxiety about doing it. I knew that if I called the doctor, all he would do was give me medicine, and that wasn't the answer. That's what the doctors wanted to do when they first saw me. Some people do need medication in some cases, but I didn't want to go that route if I didn't have to.

I think what helped me, before I got to that point, is that my sister-in-law would always say, "It's okay to get help, to go to a counselor if you need it because some people do need that." At first, I thought, *Oh, I don't need help; I can do this*, but around the holidays, the depression and the anxiety came in. When my chest started to hurt, I knew I needed to do something.

I just went out on a limb, online. I did a Google search on how to get help and on bereavement counseling and pulled up Bark.com. I put my information in. There's a lot to fill out about what kind of help you're looking for and what kind of person you might want to talk to.

I didn't even know the people I was signing up to contact, but it all worked out. God helped me to find the right people to help me. He is always there for me. At the beginning, I kind of forgot that. I questioned Him a couple of times. The thing is, at first the things I was praying for didn't get answered the way I wanted them to, but it doesn't work that way all the time.

I feel like He put me through all of this to be able to help other people. At the beginning, I thought my life was over. But He had something greater for me.

Then, the Rains Came

I remember saying a prayer before I started looking.

I started out with a grief counselor recommended through the website. The first therapist I talked to, when I told the story, she cried with me while I told it. She's still with me, too. I've got three therapists! She's since said that when she sees somebody that she can help that way, her job's worthwhile.

Then, Ron James called me. I had always asked for a female counselor, but it seemed like there was something there with Ron. The thing that stuck out to me the most was that he took his time and listened. He kept working with me to get the memories out. For a while the loss was too painful to even talk about. One time he said, "Don't you remember anything about your wife?" That's how much pain I was in.

He offered for me to come and eat out with him and some friends. I wouldn't do that because I was not very comfortable about going out in public. At that time, I was just so afraid I would end up getting COVID-19 since I had just lost my wife to it. All that uncertainty. Ron understood that and decided he would come up to see me instead. That was the best thing he could've done.

All I wanted at that time was to see people, but because of COVID, that wasn't allowed. That was hard on me. All I wanted was to be hugged and told that everything was going to be okay.

When nobody wanted to see me, Ron was the first person who actually came to the house. When he came, I was in a dark place, where my life really could have gone one way or another. I was just questioning everything. I was a little bit nervous about meeting Ron because I didn't know what to expect. Ron brought breakfast, and that was maybe the best part.

I still wasn't quite sure about how I felt after we talked, but he gave me a little hope and seemed like the right person. It was hard to share those things.

Then Ron suggested that I talk to his sister Marsan. I am so glad he did. I needed somebody to help me open up, for it just wasn't happening. What I remember the most from the first day I talked to Marsan was that she cried with me. She really understood what I was going through. We took it slow; we started talking a little bit at a time. She was able to get me to open up and share the things that were really hard for me at that time.

Not all of the memories we've talked about have been good. I have regrets. There are times I wish I'd behaved differently and things I wish I had said. Remember that the people you care about won't be here on earth forever. Don't wait. Don't stop working every day on being a better person.

Marsan told me that I would eventually look for another person to be with. At that time, it hadn't even crossed my mind. *Why would I ever want to look for another person?* I thought. But she was right.

On January 29, Debbie's birthday came around for the first time without her. I lit a candle for her and got a cupcake to eat just like it was her birthday cake. Doing those things helped get me through the day, and I am planning on continuing them as traditions.

Things were starting to get a little better. I was starting to feel pretty good by the end of the first month of 2021.

Then, my father started to have trouble breathing. The staff did the tests and found out that he had COVID, too.

The story was that he went to dialysis the morning of February 1. He had enough energy that morning to do the dialysis, but when he got back, he couldn't catch his breath. That's when they took him for tests. But my father was determined he was going to go that day.

I'd stayed in my chair the night before because Tim had called and told me that something might happen. They called me around six o'clock in the morning to tell me.

He was gone.

Dad had still been talking the night before, so I was surprised that it all happened so fast. I saw two times how quickly COVID takes a person.

The staff couldn't get in touch with Tim, so they had called me. I had to let him know.

I didn't know that I would have to be the strong one that day. I was tested, to know I could do this.

Still, it took a while for me to be able to call Tim. I tried to get all of my thoughts together before I made the call. All the questions, all the "whys" I couldn't answer for myself—I tried to get ready to answer them for Tim.

When I called, it seemed like he expected it. The conversation is a little bit of a blur in my memories. Before COVID, we'd get together after a tragedy like that, but we were still isolating then.

I was scared for myself, too, afraid that I was going to go backwards after the progress I'd made.

Debbie. Mom. My dad. All gone within ninety days.

I remember a lot of Dad's old friends, whom I had only known from church, came to the funeral. The pastor personally knew my parents and had felt like a part of the family, so it was a wonderful service. She also had worked under my brother at his first church. It was his example that had gotten her to decide to go into the ministry.

Everyone wore masks, but because it was a small country church, we were able to have something closer to a normal funeral than I'd imagine a lot of people did at that time. It felt great to be able to have that at the church the way Dad would have wanted. It was the church I'd grown up at.

So many memories were connected there. I saw a lot of people whom I hadn't seen in a long time. Tim and I had been little kids running around there once, and everybody still remembered us that way. People tell me all the time how much I look like my dad, and I heard that comment a whole lot that day.

The funeral brought back a lot of feelings, though. I was kind of a wreck that day. Trying to cry with a mask on—that's not too much fun, either!

After that, it started helping me to think about my mother. Before that, I just couldn't. I tried, but I just couldn't do it. She was like the glue for me. After all that loss, now it was like I had permission to think back and remember.

At the funeral that day, I mourned all three.

I had the three counselors at the time. Yes, I had God. But the counselors really helped me because I was upset with God in those days. I screamed and yelled at Him every night, but still I prayed.

It didn't make sense, but that was where I was at.

CHAPTER FIVE
You Are Not Alone

Looking

I wanted a friendship like I had with Debbie. I needed someone to talk to and share things with. I remember a couple of times talking about having another relationship, and it was like "*No!*"

But when you know you had that kind of love, it's hard to think about not having that anymore, and you question whether you'll have that kind of love again.

I'd like to have it again.

I still feel like I have a lot of love to give yet.

In looking for a person to love, it helps to know what you're looking for, but you have to watch that you're not trying to replace the one who is gone. You have to remember that each new person you meet is a different person.

You need to have caution.

I was looking for a friend whom I could share life with, who'd listen to me, who was caring. I think I'm a good listener, and I was ready to be there to let her share with me and to be supportive the same way I needed support.

However, I was still vulnerable when I first started to do the dating thing again, and it didn't go well with the first woman whom I connected with.

We connected on Facebook and started talking. Then this lady started telling me how much she liked me and said all of these good things. Supposedly, she was from Arizona. She had a story about how she was all alone and living with her aunt, and her aunt was so happy for her to be talking with me.

But then this woman started wanting pictures of my house and had other kinds of requests. She started to say things like, "You don't have to be alone anymore. I'll come live with you and get a job in that area." I started to get suspicious. Then she started talking about wanting to have a child with me. I thought, *We're just starting a relationship. We haven't met face to face, and you're getting into all that stuff so soon?* Personally, I think she was trying to figure out the value of the house. Maybe she was sincere and would have come like that, but then nothing good would have happened. I decided to stop talking to her.

I told Ron that story, and he suggested that I join Christian Mingle, a dating service, which is where he met his wife. At the time, we thought that would be safer. When I first got a response, I was surprised and excited at the same time—and nervous, too.

Some of what happened was my fault, too, because I just wanted a relationship so much. After only three days, this woman talked me into getting off the dating site and texting her on her own phone. I thought there was something there. At the time, I was just desperate enough that I thought, *Wow, that's pretty neat that she did that.* I know that was a mistake now, but at the time I didn't realize that.

We did a lot of talking. We could talk all day and up after midnight. She started telling me everything I wanted to hear, that she loved me and all that. She got me to start saying it, too, and then it was like I believed it.

When we're desperate, sometimes we make the wrong choices.

After, about a month into this relationship, she started wanting money. The next story was that, on her birthday, she wanted a better cell phone so she could talk to me on video rather than just calling and texting. This phone cost twelve hundred dollars, and she wanted me to send her the money for it. I listened, and that shows you how desperate I was because I wouldn't buy a cell phone for myself for that kind of money. However, I was vulnerable.

There was a lot of talk about using Paypal or a prepaid credit card to pay for it. I figure now the reason she was saying that was because if you sent money like that with the regular card, the bank would flag it and shut it down right away. She also was telling me to keep my sending her money a secret, not to tell my family or my friends.

I was getting advice to be careful with her, but those words, "I love you" ….

Ron did tell me that word *love* was messing with me because it was very important for me to hear. I wanted what I had before because I missed that. I was so desperate for a relationship that I went ahead and sent the money. I just wanted to believe her.

Then she would tell me that the cards weren't working, and she'd call me every day and cry. I was very upset.

When I look back at what happened, I see that when she started saying she loved me, it was too good to be true. At the time, I didn't see it that way, but now when I look back, I can see it. I really thought there was something there.

People around me were concerned before that point, but I wouldn't have listened anyway. When we're looking to take away some of the pain and loneliness, we can fall victim to scams. I was trying to get everything over with, thinking that I was going to get myself out of this depression. I found out that wasn't the way to do it.

The "relationship" ended badly. I don't know what her whole situation was, and I've told myself that maybe someone told her to do that, but it was still wrong. The whole thing was a learning experience, and now I try to share these lessons with others so they'll know what to stay away from.

It wasn't easy, but, after that, I decided I could try again. This time, I went on eHarmony. This time, I took more precautions and paid attention to what the guidelines told you to do. I actually followed the rules. I liked the security features on this site, as well as all the rules they had to keep me from getting into situations like the ones I did before. That safety made me confident to go back online and look for a friend.

A woman named Jeanne texted me. I was direct and to the point.

The two of us came up with an agreement. We would be friends and not hurt each other. That was in March, and we are still good friends today. At first, I was texting her morning and evening every day. At the time, she realized that I needed that connection. Marsan taught me a lot about texting, like what LOL means. I use that all the time now!

When Jeanne realized that I was starting to do things and getting a little better, she told me that we should pull back on the texting, that it was just too much. At first, that was a little hard for me, but then I talked it over with Ron and understood that it wasn't the end of something; it was just a change.

Finally I got brave enough to ask her if we could talk on the phone. She came around and said we could start doing that. It has been great. If there's anything we want to share, we text, but only once a day tops, not like before. Usually, we wait to talk about our week on Thursdays on the phone. That has helped me to have patience, too, that we can wait to tell each other things. Ron really worked with me on that.

She wants to come to my place this summer so I can grill for her. I offered to show her the mountain land where I live. Jeanne is from the country, so we understand that about each other. When I go up into the mountains, I feel most like myself, able to listen to nature. The sounds of nature give me comfort and relax me. That feeling was always kind of there, but it's stronger now. And Jeanne and I can share about our belief in God, too, which is a very good thing.

As I'm wrapping up working on this book, we've finally made our plans to meet in person for the first time.

Jeanne taught me that you have to learn to be true to yourself and to love yourself before you can have a relationship again. She lost her husband twenty years ago to cancer, and she tells me that even all of these years later, you still get some of these feelings of grief. She will tell me that sometimes she senses Deb's spirit, as if Deb wants to tell her something.

Jeanne tells me how proud she is of me for being able to get through all this emotional pain. In the beginning, I was more dependent on her, but she has seen how much more independent I have become, and we are always there for each other. When she realized that I needed to concentrate on my goals, she told me we needed to stop texting so much.

At Easter of 2021, Tim had some funerals to attend to and was still dealing with his own grief. Jeanne encouraged me to keep reaching out to him. She knew I wouldn't have family around that holiday, so she told me all about what her family was doing that day. I felt like I was part of it. She did it because she went through the same thing, and I knew that. The thing I remember about Easter is that most of the people I talked to were all my new friends. I thought that was something. I remembered how, years ago, I sat all alone in the school cafeteria. Now I had all these people God had brought into my life.

I remember telling Jeanne that I just wanted the grief to be over. She told me that I couldn't do that. I needed to take my time and get to know myself, too. And I am learning more about myself every day. It did make sense, but sometimes you just want all this emotional pain to be gone.

On the other hand, having that emotion means you loved that person. I took a while to accept it, but Debbie is better off where she is now; she has no more pain and suffering. But I'll never forget her love. That's never going to happen.

I think the most important thing about my relationship with my wife Debbie is that my love for her was real, and it's still there. People might worry if they will keep that love or forget it in another relationship. My love for my wife—it's always going to be with me, and I can visit it whenever I want. If I have another relationship, I want that other person to understand that.

The thing I learned is that I can have friendship and companionship and everything doesn't have to be about leading to marriage or the same thing I had before. Sometimes I have to remind myself to be patient in a relationship and see what happens because I will want things that maybe I can't have right now. When it's my time, love will come.

Like Marsan says, we want the right people in our life, not just anybody. And I know now that any relationship I have, it has to be for me first.

For every time I gave Deb that little nudge, she's giving it back to me now.

One Day at a Time

That saying is something my wife taught me.

One day at a time.

It's what she'd say in the nursing home.

One day at a time.

I remember those words. Always remember the words our loved ones had for us; hang onto them.

What I've been though, it makes me appreciate life more now.

From the beginning, I wanted to be able to share my experience. I was praying to God for answers, but I wouldn't get the answer each time. I guess He was waiting for the right time.

Sometimes, it's worth the wait.

The sunrise and sunset … I enjoy watching them now. And taking pictures. Another thing I've started to do is drive up the mountain and listen to nature, turning off all the machines and just hearing. Sometimes you've got to stop what you're doing and just listen.

I like being outside, seeing the birds and being able to take pictures of beautiful scenery—especially in the spring when everything starts to get green. I like being able to go up in the mountains, shut off and just listen to nature. It just gives us a closer connection to God, I think.

One thing I try to make a point of doing is looking for things to take pictures of, such as the wildlife and the sunrise and sunset. I put the pictures on Facebook and share them. I wanted somebody to share them with, and that was a good way to do it. It was a way to stay connected. My first grief counselor suggested the idea. There are so many good things to take pictures of, and hobbies like that can give you something to look forward to and to share with others.

Stop and smell the roses. There's a red rose bush that still grows outside our house that Debbie planted. I had to trim it back a little to stop it from peeking in through the bedroom window.

I've grown in my faith—and learned more about my faith, too. After loving my wife for twenty-four years and going through the last couple of months, I remembered how she had that faith in God and was just positive. Debbie had two amputation surgeries, but she was positive the whole time.

I still go to church every Sunday, and I love being able to share with my friends at church. I like to do the Bible studies, too.

Our church had a Facebook page and used that to keep in touch with everyone during COVID, when we weren't able to have a physical service. I logged in there every week for the video service. That helped get me connected back to God after what happened. It takes a little bit of time after you experience that kind of tragedy. You start questioning things.

In church, you talk to everyone before the service very easily. But then, during COVID, a lot of the time the service was on Zoom. The church would do a lot of praying for me, too, which I always appreciated. I asked people for some help, but probably not as much as I should have.

I remember a particularly rough morning, right after my father died, when I was in the church Zoom session. I was sitting there listening to the service and looked out the window when three cardinals flew in and landed right there on the deck. Looking at them really brought me peace that day. I remembered how I'd seen a cardinal the day I got to sleep for the first time after Debbie passed, too.

There's a long tradition of cardinals reminding us of the loved ones we've lost. Some people believe they actually ferry the souls back to visit us; others believe that they're there to remind us to remember.

Three hard losses those last few months.

And three cardinals landed there on my deck.

I remember texting the church's Facebook page about it afterwards. Pastor Rachel, who takes care of that page, texted back and said, "Wow!" Not one. Not two. But *three*. People who watch their cardinals all the time told me you might see two, but you never see three cardinals together.

I figured it was a sign. It encouraged me. God comforted me through them that morning.

To this day, when I have a bad day, I'll notice a cardinal nearby.

And I remember.

At the time, Pastor Rachel would be online and members could share how they were feeling. I shared a lot of things with her, and she would answer back. A lot of church members would respond, too, because they knew I was having a hard time, and they made sure that they chimed in. I know that was a big help for me.

I just recently started going back to church in person, and it's been going really well. The first Sunday when the first hymn came up, I got a little emotional. I prayed to God in order to calm down a little. The best part of going back to church was getting to hear the organ again, like when Mom used to play. It just wasn't the same to hear it at home over the internet.

Going back was a big step. It was important, though, because ever since my wife died, I've wanted to be back in church again. Debbie was a big part of the church. Going on Sunday was what we did.

We lost a lot of members to COVID this year, and it was kind of hard to not see them there.

My faith in God helps me to keep going and helps me to know that there's something better out there. Also, that my wife and my parents family are in a better place now.

God told me to hold on through those birds.

The next thing I did was join my first Bible study on Facebook, through UCC. That really helped with what I was going through at the time. A lot of those people talked about COVID, too, because it was affecting them. I got to hear the other side because there was a nurse who would talk about how she felt. Some of the people participating weren't even members of our church. They were from different areas and would join our group. My pastor had been a pastor in Hawaii for a while, and one of the members from there was part of our group. Her sister helped out, too.

It started as just being a Bible study, not so much a group to help people through these hard times. But that's what it ended up being. Every week when I was with the group on Zoom, I felt like He was talking to me. Other people there said the same thing.

We also did something that was kind of like an art thing, where you could express how you felt about the Bible verses. It wasn't just what the pictures were about; it was how you felt about them, so it didn't have to be perfect. There's one I drew about the path, the path of moving on. I think I called it "Moving Toward the Sun." That was how I drew that. I kept that one.

I also was attending a support group in a church in Chambersburg. That really helped, too, to talk things out. There are just different ways to handle grief, and you see that with other people. One time, when I went to the support group, a new person was there. I was talking about losing my parents, and she said, "I don't have my parents anymore, either." Her husband had died as well. I didn't get the whole story there yet. But this person may come back later and we'll learn more. It might be too early for this woman to talk about all of it. Everyone takes his or her own time.

There's a bit of fogginess after a loss. Sometimes you forget to eat or drink. Sometimes I'd eat only one meal a day. The first time I made chili, I made a little too much. I was like, *What am I going to do with all this?* I ended up giving Sweetie some of the chili. It helps to share.

It's starting to get easier to remember now. For a while, I couldn't tell stories like I have here. I've started to remember the happy moments now. I can look at the pictures now—that's gotten easier. I'll look at the pictures of my wife sometimes and wonder, *What was she thinking about?*

The first Mother's Day and Father's Day without my parents were hard. You look at Facebook and see everybody talking about their mom and dad. Sometimes it helps to get off Facebook, too.

I've been thinking about the idea that sharing my parents with all of you is the best Mother's Day and Father's Day gifts I can give them—keeping them alive through the stories.

I was listening to this radio station one time, and they made a good point that, on Mother's Day, you should remember people who don't have their mothers and reach out and talk to them. The radio people suggested finding your mom's favorite flower and giving it to someone else or finding a place to put it. You can think of other memories and share them with people. You can tell stories about your mom—and remind people to tell their mother they love her.

When I texted Jeanne—she's a mother—I told her to have a good Mother's Day. She really appreciated that. It's nice to say it to someone.

My father used to like to have a cookout on Father's Day. It was important to have the family together; that was his big thing.

My friend helped me put a deck on the back of the house. In the beginning, I wasn't really excited about it. *I'm by myself. Why would I want that deck?* That was the first thing that went through my mind. But, one day, people will want to come up. Besides, there was Ron, grilling steaks on my birthday. I promised him that one day we'll have to do steaks for him! I know he has family, and still he went out of his way to do that for me.

Jeanne sent me a card with a cross in it. She also sent me a video singing "Happy Birthday" to me, and then she called and said "Happy Birthday" again.

Things like that helped me.

I keep a picture of Debbie and me together that I look at now. Sometimes, it can be heavy, emotionally, to look at pictures, but I keep going.

When Debbie's birthday came around on January 29, 2021, I donated to my church in her memory. I thought that could be a gift for her and maybe help somebody else, too. I also donated her coat to the church. Knowing that her coat would keep someone else warm made me feel better. In the winter, her love is wrapped around somebody else.

I recently started talking more to Pastor Rachel, which helps a lot. There are some things she knows about me because she had been around Debbie and I for so long. She knows the relationship Deb and I had. She was there the whole time through all of Debbie's health problems, and that made me trust her. Knowing everything I lost and not knowing where to go afterwards for a while made me feel weak. When I talked to my pastor, she helped to pull me out of that.

COVID wasn't done with me yet, unfortunately. Aunt Helen passed away in the spring. It was good that my brother led that service because he could tell memories of his aunt. I'm sure it helped him, too. Even when we were adults, she still called us Timmy and Jimmy. We were still kids to her! Lots of good memories were shared at that funeral.

I want to be able to honor my family. They wouldn't want me to grieve for the rest of my life; they would want me to enjoy it. But there is a season for grief, and they would want me to get through that. Some people mourn longer than others, and that's okay, too.

I have learned that you have to take your time.

Take it one day at a time.

The Future

> *more like the people*
> *we wanted to be*
> *we were called to be*
> *we hoped to be*[8]

I've been trying to find ways to start thinking ahead again. For a long time, I kept thinking back about everything. Things happen, but you can still come around, choose life and start looking ahead.

I want to see my nephew graduate—that's my goal. My mother always wanted to see his graduation; I want to fight so I can see it. Andrew is sixteen. It's not going to be long now. It will be important to him to have me there.

It's important to fight for those who still need us.

I started exercising. I go to the gym now. It's working out well for me. I have changed the way I eat, and I'm feeling good about that, too. Luckily with my diet, I can still eat protein bars with chocolate, so I can satisfy that craving. I had to give up a lot of other foods, like rolls and all that bread.

One big thing I do now, if I go out and eat, I make sure to tip the waitresses. I know they're working hard with everything that's going on.

Stop and remember what others do every day.

At one restaurant, I saw where people weren't giving the waitresses much, and then I made my waitress's day by giving her a tip. With one person, you don't expect it to be that much, so she was really surprised. I do that because I want to make somebody's day.

Make somebody else's day whenever you can.

I remember the first time I went out to eat by myself. That wasn't easy. I started to realize that usually the waitress would talk to you, and that helps a little bit. Sometimes just being around people, even if you are out by yourself, helps.

In the beginning, you couldn't do that because of COVID. That's why I came up with other things to do. The drive-thrus were open then. I did a lot of that. You didn't really have any kind of social re-

---

8 Laura Kelly Fanucci, "When This Is Over," as quoted in Zachary Willette, "This COVID-19 Poem Says So Much," Allay Care blog, March 30, 2020. https://www.allaycare.org/blog/2020/3/30/when-this-is-over-a-reflection-on-the-little-things.

lationships at the time, and I really wanted that, even if it was just briefly talking to somebody.

I've had to relearn how to do some things on my own. What I used to do when shopping with my wife is put items in her basket when she was using the Walmart scooter. After she died, I had to learn to shop by myself. But I was determined to keep going. I saw what it looks like when a person loses independence when my wife lost hers. I don't want that to happen to me. But, she fought for her independence as long as she could.

The last couple of months I've learned to get better with computers so I could contact people. Before, I didn't even know how to text. Now I can type things on the phone. I'm still learning about Zoom.

I've met some great people along this journey. Sometimes I think back and am surprised I made these friends on my own.

Ron has become a good friend. He always tells me that I can improve myself and do better for myself than what I am now. He's very supportive of me, always believing that I can accomplish things. Looking at his life and reading the book he wrote shows me that if you have faith in God, then you can accomplish those things. And he's always got my back.

Ron invited me into his family, so I kind of feel like part of his family. A little while ago, I got to spend some time with Ron and his daughter Mireya. She inspires me, too, as she has a handicap but can really get around. Ron has really been like a brother to me.

I've been able to check off one item from my bucket list this year: Ron and I went to a NASCAR race at the Pocono Raceway, the Pocono Organics 325, on June 26. He shared with me that it was something he always wanted to do, too, so it all worked out. At first, I couldn't watch NASCAR because that was something else Debbie and I did together. It was good to be able to reconnect with it this way.

I have a "can-do" list of things I want to get out and accomplish and seeing a NASCAR race was high on it. There's a lot still out there yet to see.

One thing I found about NASCAR is watching it in person is not like watching it on TV. The track is huge! You can't actually see down to the other end. That was really surprising to me. I also was just impressed with how a race car can go from one hundred miles per hour down to something like forty miles per hour in a heartbeat. I wonder how you do that!

Just being able to spend that time with Ron was fun. I can't wait to go back and do it again.

Another thing that really meant a lot to me was that Marsan and I went on a trip together. To be able to travel meant a lot. I appreciate that she was able to point out some things about driving and how to correct that for me. She showed me that I can do those things again and be able to enjoy my life again and travel. It's my dream to get back on the road and travel like that again.

I love that we work together and that I can share things like this now. She told me that I could get to this point where I am now. I didn't really believe that at first, but she was right. Marsan is just a great friend; she's like the sister I never had. I know she'll always be there for me.

It's good to have things to do when I get up in the morning now. One of my therapists reminds me of when I wanted to be busy like I am now. It's good to be grateful.

Stages
I'm sure you've heard of the "Five Stages of Grief." Bereavement therapists had noticed these patterns since the 1940s, but the Five Stages model is usually credited to Elisabeth Kübler-Ross, who wrote about it in her 1969 book *On Death and Dying*.

The stages don't always come in the same order, and you can go back and forth between them. But for me, they looked like this:

1. Denial
At first, I was in shock, trying to deny what had happened. I went numb as I tried to make it through one day at a time during this phase. Doing so actually helps, because it allows us to work through our grief at our own pace.

The first day I just wanted to be by myself, to tell myself it hadn't happened. That I was going to wake up from a dream and everything was going to be okay. Part of that sitting for three hours in the hospital was just hoping that it was all a mistake and that she was going to wake up again.

I was just feeling, *What am I going to do without her?* I couldn't even think it was real. This wasn't part of the plan.

I didn't really want help then, not like when I realized I needed it later, because I thought if I did ask for help, people would just make me face what I'd lost, over and over. I didn't want that. I wanted to stay numb to the reality of it.

2. Anger
You'll feel a lot of emotions later, but at first, it's mostly just anger—anger with God, anger with yourself, anger with anyone who passes your way. It's important to feel this anger. God gave you and me those emotions for a reason, and it's okay to lean on them, even when it hurts. The more you feel it, the more it will pass, and you can get to the other feelings underneath.

I told people the hole I put in the wall with the scooter was an accident, but it wasn't. I meant to do it. It was hard to hear that news, and I had to lash out. It took a little while for the nurse to get around to telling me what happened, and everything that happened after she told me was just a fog.

When I first went out in the world, small things like someone parking me in would make me so angry. I would scream and rage. I did that because I was angry about everything else. Afterwards, I'd ask myself why I was angry; it was just stupid. I can laugh now about some of the things I was upset about then, but at the time it was so hard.

3. Bargaining
It's easy to get lost in "What if?" and offer God all kinds of changes in your life if He'll only take things back to the way they were.

I did so much of this bargaining when Debbie was sick. I negotiated with God, trying to make a deal. I made so many promises about how I'd be better, do better, if He'd just let her come home.

4. Depression
This stage is when you feel empty, when the numbness and anger start to go away and you really start to feel the grief. It feels like it will last

forever. It's important to remember, though, that this is not mental illness presenting itself. Rather, it's the process of feeling that great loss you've lived through. And you do need to feel it.

It will get better, but it won't go away. And it will only happen at your own pace. You have to learn to love that person another way when he or she is gone. I was able to grieve at my own pace, but a lot of that was because of COVID. There wasn't anybody around to do anything with to get tired of my problems.

I do remember one Sunday when I went out to lunch with family and tried to talk about Deb and everybody got quiet. They didn't know what to do. I was starting to feel like I was ready to share at that time, but it can be uncomfortable for people to be around those who are grieving. They want to change the subject.

I hope if you're reading this book and you haven't lost someone but know someone who has, that you'll read this story and know not to run from that person's grief. He or she needs your support and needs to talk about the memories. Three months after. Six months after. Even now, a year after, it's nice to have people check in on me.

I know people's grief can be hard to face. I know I ran myself when I didn't know how to be with people when they were suffering. But it helps so much when you just listen. Let people share. It helps.

5. Acceptance

Acceptance does not mean that things finally become "okay." Everything has changed, and you have to finally accept the new normal of your life. You will never like what has changed, but to move on, you must come to terms with it.

I'm a different person today than I was before. I think I'm a better person than I was. My faith is a large part of that.

I can pray and know that God is there for me now. If I'm having a hard day, I can pray and know that He's there for me. He was always there for me. I didn't always think that, but He was always there.

If you're going through a rough patch, God is still there. You have to keep listening, keep praying. You will get your answers. He helped me through other people and through the Bible studies. The answers came through the things He sent into my life.

Have patience.
Keep praying.
Keep listening.

You have to want to listen. The answers won't come in your time. They'll come in His time, as part of His plan.

That's another thing you have to accept.

Hope in Challenging Times

Mom gave me a good home, a good outlook on life. She taught me to be more positive and more supportive of other people. Dad gave me knowledge. I can't do the things myself that he could, but he taught me to do some of the minor repairs around the house. I also know what people are talking about when they come to work on the house, so I don't get taken advantage of. Debbie gave me an example of how to fight through incredible hardship. She was positive and fought the whole way. When her leg was amputated. With COVID. And she showed me what unfailing love is.

I am grateful for my loving parents as well as for my relationship with my brother. I am very grateful that I had twenty-four loving years with my wife.

They will always be with me in my heart.

I fought to go on after Debbie and Mom and Dad died because I knew that's what they'd want, for me to enjoy my life again. They all were instrumental in my life, and now I am going to prove to everyone how important they were by trusting in the things I was taught.

I'm still doing the little things every day because I want to get better. I want to be a better person.

I have a "toolbox" filled with tools from my father. My mother. My grandparents. My pastors. My wife. I just have to reach down and pick up the right tool.

I know they're cheering me on, every step of the way.

At first, the quiet was hard, but I've gotten to be okay with it, even to appreciate it. It is time to relax and just be.

Sometimes you just need to have time with God, too. He's there to talk with you any time you need Him. My faith helped me, and that was introduced to me when I was a small child. I think some of the people in church can see that difference in me now, too. It helped me to have some comfort and peace.

But there are still tough days. The grief can hit in waves.

If you're feeling this way, you're not alone. These feelings are normal, and you have to experience them for yourself. I've learned that you can't hold them in; you have to cry and let them out to create a space to breathe. Sometimes I shout and yell them out. Other times, I don't know what to do. Then a phone call will come and connect me again.

I had to be determined and push through, however. It was a fight every single day.

Get them out. Cry them out. Let them go. That's how we get through.

I did the work, but the support was there because I asked for it. Reach out for the help. You're not going to do it on your own. You have to take your time. You can't rush everything.

I learned that it's a good thing to remember the ones who are gone. Talking about the grief, sharing it, helped. Having someone listen. Another thing I learned through this is that I have more friends than I thought I had. I didn't always realize that. Reaching out to make friends is a big thing. We need people to talk to. I think sometimes that it helps me when I think of somebody else.

But, you have to do the work. A person can encourage you, but you have to do the work. You have to push yourself. I still have to do that some days. It all comes back to your own thoughts.

I think, when I looked in the mirror and didn't like what I saw, when I didn't see my smile, I wanted to get that back. It took a long time to get that. I wanted to have that smile. I was going through so much that I didn't feel like smiling anymore.

I think, through all this, I started to love myself more than I did before. I put myself out there more than I used to, too. That was a hard place to get to, though. I think going through this makes you connect more to yourself than you used to.

I think I was helping my wife all the time and not thinking about myself much.

She would want me to be happy again. I know there are going to be hard days yet, but I think I could tell Debbie now that I'm okay.

This part of my life is about telling my story and helping other people. More than anything, I want people to know who my loved ones were and how I was able to go through the pain of their loss. I would never have thought I could do any of that in the beginning.

I am really excited about being a life coach now. It's a chance for me to share what I've learned. By talking about my experience and telling you how I got through it, I hope I can help. Spread hope whenever you can, and it will come back to you when you need it.

I like to share what I call my "Five Reasons for Hope in Challenging Times":

1. Grieving Takes Time
The grieving process can last months for some and years for others. Over time, it gets easier to cope with grief as you learn new skills to heal. Practice self-care every day.

2. Time Changes Life
If there is one constant in life, it is change. Things may seem bleak now, but in a year your situation may be different. Think of times when you faced hardships and your life improved afterwards.

3. Grief Is Common
When you experience loss, it can feel like you are isolated and alone. But humankind has been struggling with grief for as long as we have existed. Fortunately, help is easier to find now than it has been in the past. Talk to a loved one about your grief.

4. Healing Isn't Linear
Healing from loss isn't a process where you continue to make positive progress toward healing every day. It's more like a cycle. You will have good days and bad days. The skills you learn will help lessen the impact of the bad days. Think of something you are grateful for.

5. Help Is Always Available
From different studies of grief, we are better able to treat it today than we were one hundred years ago. No matter what your preferred style of

therapy is, there is sure to be a right fit out there. Do something today to find help.

I have more peace with knowing that my parents, who loved and served the Lord all their lives, are with their Heavenly Father. They loved, helped, provided and lived the best lives they knew how. It is easier to accept the comfort He offered about their lives and where they are now.

I find comfort in that today.

Realizing that Debbie wasn't in all that pain anymore and that she was with her Father in heaven was a big part of my coming to acceptance. People told me that over and over, but I didn't want to hear it. I needed to come to that knowledge on my own.

When people leave this world, they don't take their things with them. Debbie's clothes, her collections, all her earthly things, are still here. She left her pain behind, too, as well as her sorrows and her disappointments. She didn't need any of that where she has gone. And she left something else behind, too, something she left for me. In fact, it's the same thing she took with her: love. The ones we've lost have left love behind for us once we are ready to accept it.

For a long time, I felt guilty for yelling at her on that last day. But she didn't take that with her. And I have to let it go, too.

The one thing that felt better right away was the fact that I didn't have to worry about her anymore. But then I felt guilty about that! It was my job to worry. I was glad not to have to worry, but I felt like I was missing a part of myself, the part that worried for Debbie.

I had to start looking forward, setting goals and thinking about the future, not looking back to those worries that God had already taken care of. Helping other people is what I most wanted to do. When you understand other people's pain, it is important to do something with that knowledge.

I often think back to that children's song, "Jesus Love Me." It still sticks with me, all those years after Sunday school. Mom played the piano, and Dad taught us the words. When I was a kid, I often wondered why I had to go to church, why they made me go. Now, when they're not here, that foundation that they gave me, the ability to talk to God and receive His guidance, means more to me than ever.

God sent people into my life, friends whom I needed.
My faith, my trust in God—I will always have that to go to.
I fight.
I live.
To be able to reach others.

God's going to be the One who is always there for you. You can't look for that faith through another person. I tried that, but it doesn't work. You need that foundation inside first, and that comes through faith.

It's okay to give. It's okay to receive.

Life is not an easy road. You have to fight. But it's worth it. For me, it's worth it now. You never know what's on the other side.

* * *

I remember.

I remember sitting around the campfire with my family after the campground store closed for the night. S'mores and stories.

I remember the "haunted hayride," as a thirty-year-old man on my very first date. Jumping into Debbie's arms.

I remember the words, "You may kiss the bride," and a magical kiss that seemed to go on forever.

I remember Easter with the whole family: Mom and Dad, me and Tim, and everyone who'd come into our lives. All together.

I remember sitting in the hospital room with Debbie, laughing at Deputy Sheriff Barney Fife. Being together, even when things were hard.

I remember it all, and those memories will always be with me. Mom, Dad and Debbie will always be in my heart. I thank God for every day I had with them.

And I promise to never stop fighting to make them proud.

Like Debbie said, one day at a time.

www.ingramcontent.com/pod-product-compliance
Lightning Source LLC
Chambersburg PA
CBHW052109110526
44592CB00013B/1535